Cycling
the Erie Canal

A guide to 400 miles
of adventure and history
along the Erie Canalway Trail

Published by

Parks & Trails
N E W Y O R K

Every effort has been made to make this guide as accurate and useful as possible. However, many things can change after publication – names of establishments, phone numbers, websites, and, in this case, the Canalway Trail itself, as more and more miles are completed over the next few years.

Please check the Parks & Trails website — www.ptny.org — for a current list of updates to the guide and to submit corrections. While visiting our website, we encourage you to register in our on-line guest book and share your discoveries and insights about the Canalway Trail. You may also submit comments and corrections by mail to: PTNY Cycling Guide, 29 Elk Street, Albany, NY 12207.

ISBN 0-9748277-0-3
Printed in the United States
2004

Parks & Trails New York
29 Elk Street
Albany, NY 12207
www.ptny.org
ptny@ptny.org
518-434-1583

Use of this guide and its information is at the user's own risk.

**WE WISH TO ACKNOWLEDGE
THE GENEROUS FINANCIAL SUPPORT
OF THE FOLLOWING AGENCIES
AND ORGANIZATIONS
THAT MADE THIS
PUBLICATION POSSIBLE**

New York State Canal Corporation

Erie Canalway National Heritage
Corridor Commission

New York State Council
on the Arts, a State Agency

The Business Council
of New York State, Inc.

New York State Department of Health

Health Research, Inc.

Centers for Disease Control
and Prevention
U50CCU22133302

*A special thank you
to New York State Senator
George D. Maziarz,
New York's "Canal Senator,"
for his support
of Parks & Trails New York
and his abiding affection for
and belief in the future
of New York's canal system.*

TABLE OF CONTENTS

TABLE OF CONTENTS

INTRODUCTION

Welcome to the Erie Canalway Trail! The trail route follows both active and historic sections of the Erie Canal, the renowned inland waterway that opened the frontier of the fledgling United States to settlement and commerce, transforming the nation in the process.

The Erie Canalway Trail is very much a work in progress. For more than 20 years, state and local governments have been transforming old towpath and abandoned rail corridor into multi-use pathways. Currently, about 60 percent of the off-road route is in place, with 2007 targeted for completion of the entire trail. New trail segments and improvements to existing segments are scheduled over the next few years. Users of this guide should consult the Parks & Trails New York website, www.ptny.org, or the NYS Canal Corporation website, www.canals.state.ny.us, for updates and links to information on trail progress and construction-related closings and detours.

HOW TO USE THIS GUIDE

The *Cycling the Erie Canal* guidebook is primarily designed for use by bicyclists, but it will also be useful to those enjoying the trail on foot or by other means. It is divided into three primary sections: Overview, Maps, and Services. Additional information on cycling safety, travel, and logistics is also included.

Overview

This section provides basic information about the Erie Canalway Trail and the history of the Erie Canal corridor.

Maps

The 42 full-color maps constitute the core of the guide. Four types of maps are included: overview, section, detail, and downtown inset. The map pages have colored borders, with the colors corresponding to particular sections. For example, all the detail maps in the first section from Buffalo to Rochester have green borders. Both the section and detail maps are numbered in ascending order from west to east. The pages opposite the maps contain information on points of interest and services, as well as some interpretive information.

Overview map

The overview map shows the location of the trail corridor within New York State relative to major geographic features and transportation gateways. It also depicts the coverage of the section maps.

Section maps

The four 90-mile section maps show the location of the trail corridor relative to major- and moderate-size communities and include transportation information. They also depict the areas covered in the detail maps as color-coded, numbered boxes. The section maps and their corresponding detail maps are color-coded as follows:

- Section 1: Buffalo to Rochester   green
- Section 2: Rochester to Syracuse   brown
- Section 3: Syracuse to Little Falls   blue
- Section 4: Little Falls to Albany   red

Detail maps and downtown insets

The 33 detail maps each cover an area of roughly 10 miles by 5 miles, centered along the trail corridor. They identify trailhead and parking areas as well as points of interest and services. In addition, four of the detail maps have shaded boxes that indicate downtown inset maps. The inset maps are labeled with the number of the detail map in which they are found, followed by an 'A' (e.g.1A). Most of the detail maps are horizontal, keeping with the general alignment of the Erie Canalway Trail. However, for easier reading, a few have a vertical orientation.

Services

Lodging

This section contains information for the lodging facilities marked on the detail maps. Lodging facilities are grouped according to the detail map on which they appear, then by type of lodging – B&B, motel, and campground.

Bike shops

This section contains information for bike shops located within a reasonable ride of the Erie Canalway Trail. Shops that offer bicycle rentals are indicated.

Fairs and festivals

This section contains a listing of fairs and festivals in communities along the Erie Canalway Trail arranged by time of year so you can check to see if something special is happening during your visit.

OVERVIEW

About the Erie Canalway Trail

The approximately 380-mile Erie Canalway Trail route runs east-west between the cities of Albany and Buffalo in upstate New York. Along the way, it links the cities of Rochester, Syracuse, Rome, Utica, and Schenectady.

The trail is mostly level with an average grade of 1%, since it primarily follows canal and rail corridors. There are a few steeper grades and hills (climbs greater than 400 feet), mostly in the Mohawk River Valley, but they should not pose a serious barrier even for the novice cyclist.

Surface

The off-road segments of the Erie Canalway Trail route have different surfaces. Most of the trail is surfaced in stone dust, although there are significant paved sections and a few "natural" segments.

The stone dust surface is comprised of crushed limestone, which, when compacted and dry, is hard like pavement and is universally accessible. However, when newly installed or wet, it can 'grab' the narrow wheels of touring and racing bicycles and wheelchairs. Wheeled users should use caution under the above conditions. Because stone dust is the most common surface type, wide tires are preferable for all types of bicycles and the use of a hybrid or mountain bike with non-knobby tires is recommended.

The asphalt surfacing is similar to most paved roads. A few paved trail segments have bumpy sections where tree roots have pushed up the surface. Use caution in these stretches.

Natural surfacing basically means that the old towpath or rail corridor has been cleared of trees and brush. The trail tread along many of the natural segments is rutted and lined with roots. Persons riding bikes that aren't equipped with wider tires and shocks or suspension will find these sections uncomfortable to ride at anything much above a walking pace and may want to seek out alternate on-road options.

Getting to the trail

Visitors can reach the Erie Canal corridor by several means of transportation. Check the travel and logistics section of the guide for detailed tips and ideas for getting to and from the trail.

Four international airports serve the corridor. In addition, numerous airfields and small public airports are located along the corridor within a modest bicycle ride of the Erie Canalway Trail.

Nine Amtrak stations provide rail service along a route that generally parallels that of the canal and offers links to New York City, Toronto, Montreal, Cleveland, Chicago, and Boston.

Long-distance bus lines serve most of the larger cities along the route. Greyhound and Trailways are the two main ticketing companies.

The New York State Thruway (I-90) roughly parallels the canal and is the primary artery for automotive travel through the region.

The Erie Canalway Trail is, for the most part, easy to access, with numerous trailheads with formalized parking space. Most of these trailheads and parking areas are shown on the guide detail maps. Many of the locks and lift bridges operated by the New York State Canal Corporation also have parking areas. If you don't see signs indicating designated parking at these locations, be sure to check with the attendants.

Many trailheads present no major barriers to the disabled or are intentionally designed to be universally accessible for those using wheelchairs. These trailheads are indicated with a special symbol on the maps.

Downtown areas of cities and medium to large villages usually have designated parking areas. However, these areas are frequently limited to short-term parking. Be sure to check the posted parking regulations before setting out on your trip. In large cities, paid parking lots close to the trail route are often the most convenient and secure options; many of these are also marked on the detail maps. If you plan to stay overnight at hotels or B&B's, you might also ask to use their parking facilities.

Larger urban and suburban areas usually have regional transit systems that can be used to reach trail access points. Many of these systems are equipped to carry bicycles as well as pedestrians. Call visitor information centers to obtain numbers for local transit agencies.

Weather

For cyclists and walkers, May through September offers the best weather for an extended trip on the Erie Canalway Trail. June, July, and August tend to be the sunniest and driest months. Summer precipitation often means short but powerful thunderstorms with heavy rain. Spring and fall rain showers tend to be lighter, but last longer. The chart below shows basic seasonal weather data averaged for the whole corridor:

Month	Mar-Apr	May	Jun	Jul	Aug	Sep	Oct-Nov	Dec-Feb
Hi Temp	50	68	77	82	79	72	54	33
Lo Temp	31	46	55	60	59	51	37	17
Relative Humidity	57	54	56	55	58	61	63	68
Wind Speed	11	10	9	9	8	8	10	11
Wind Direction	W	W	NW	NW	W	W	SW	W
Percent Possible Sunshine	50%	57%	63%	66%	63%	57%	40%	36%
Days With Any Precipitation	44%	41%	37%	33%	33%	36%	43%	49%

For more accurate conditions and forecasts, visit the National Weather Service homepage (www.nws.noaa.gov) and look up the weather for Buffalo, Rochester, Syracuse, Utica, or Albany. Cross-country skiers may be interested to know that the western and central portions of the trail corridor get the most average snowfall: Buffalo & Rochester – 91 inches; Syracuse – 115 inches; Albany – 64 inches. Some sections of the Canalway Trail permit snowmobile use. Always be familiar with the regulations of the section of the trail you are using.

Multi-day trips

This guide is particularly useful for persons who are taking multi-day trips or who plan to travel the entire length of the Erie Canalway Trail. The maps are organized from west to east because the prevailing westerly winds make this direction the path of least resistance for a long-distance cycling trip.

An average of approximately 40 miles per day allows significant daily progress, while ensuring time to visit many of the interesting sites along the route. At this rate, it would take roughly nine or 10 days to travel the whole Erie Canalway Trail from Buffalo to Albany. For cyclists who don't have the time to ride the entire trail in one trip, the guide has been divided into four roughly equal sections. Each section is about 90 miles long, a length that can easily be cycled over the course of a long weekend, including travel time to and from the trail. Of course, you can break down your adventure along the canal into whatever grouping of days and distances works best for you.

A brief history of the Erie Canal

The New York State Canal System is the most commercially enduring and historically significant canalway in the United States. This historic waterway played a key role in turning New York City into a major port and New York State into a preeminent center for commerce, industry, and finance.

Besides being a catalyst for growth in the Mohawk and Hudson valleys, New York's canals helped open up western America for settlement and, for many years, transported much of the Midwest's agricultural and industrial products to domestic and international markets.

The canals facilitated not only the movement of people but the spread of ideas and social reforms such as the abolition of slavery and the advocacy of women's rights.

A grand vision

Starting in the late 1700s, numerous citizens from the Northeast and immigrants from Europe headed to the unsettled lands of the American West to make new lives for themselves. Many of them followed the Mohawk River because it provided one of the better avenues through the Appalachian Mountains despite rapids and falls requiring difficult portages.

Soon, George Washington and others were envisioning canals that would link the Hudson River with Lake Champlain and the Great Lakes to enhance north-south commerce and create an east-west trade route in the United States.

In 1792, New York chartered a company to build canals and, under the direction of Revolutionary War General Philip Schuyler, went to work making some navigational improvements. Subsequent efforts failed to gain federal support for a "Great Western" canal so New York, led by Governor De Witt Clinton, decided to go ahead on its own.

Ground was broken on the Erie Canal on July 4, 1817. Though no state had undertaken such a large physical and financial project, work progressed rapidly as American laborers and newly arrived Europeans dug trenches, moved rock, and built locks by hand, while engineers developed and refined new construction techniques and materials. Crews were assembled to work simultaneously on three sections of the 348-mile Erie Canal, so large portions could operate before the entire canal was completed in 1825, two years after completion of the Champlain Canal.

An immediate success

The canals were an immediate success as processions of canal boats traveled back and forth transporting passengers and all sorts of goods, especially lumber and grain. For the first time, commerce between the Atlantic states and the Midwest had become practical. Now New York State was attracting much of the traffic that formerly moved east along the Saint Lawrence River or south along the Mississippi River.

Within 20 years, tolls had paid off construction costs of the original Erie

Canal and communities were springing up from Albany to Buffalo. "Clinton's Ditch" became known as the "Mother of Cities." Many of these cities and towns continue to show the influence of the canals today.

The Erie Canal also quickly gained an international reputation as a 19th century engineering marvel, a symbol of American ingenuity, growth, and progress. Europeans taking a Grand Tour visited the canal, along with such natural wonders as the Hudson River Valley and Niagara Falls.

The Erie's success sparked other canal projects in several eastern states. By 1877, New York alone had 907 miles of canal with 565 locks, including laterals connecting with the Erie.

A slow decline as competition grew

The Erie and other canals in the United States soon faced strong competition from the railroads, which could move freight and passengers much faster than the mule-powered canal boats that traveled two or three miles per hour. By 1868, the New York Central and Erie railroads carried a combined tonnage greater than the New York canals.

Motors replaced mules, locks were enlarged, and other improvements were made to the canals over the years, but the railroads prevailed. Then, in the latter half of the 20th century, cars, trucks, highways, airplanes, and the Saint Lawrence Seaway drew progressively more commercial traffic away from the New York State Canal System.

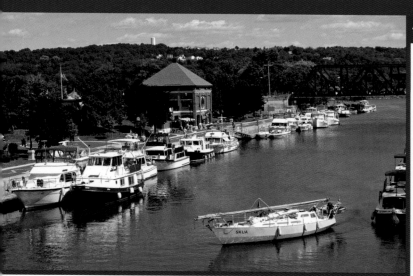

Revitalization of the Canal

In 1995, after an intensive three-year effort, the state, under the direction of the NYS Canal Corporation, produced the New York State Canal Recreationway Plan. The plan proposed a revitalization of the canal system by preserving major historical features, protecting natural settings, enhancing recreational opportunities, and fostering economic development.

Major components of the plan are well underway, including a network of canal landings to attract and serve visitors, expansion of boating activities, a scenic auto route along the canals, and development of an end-to-end Canalway Trail.

National prominence once again

In recognition of the canal system's national significance, the U.S. Congress designated the Erie Canalway National Heritage Corridor in 2000. The Heritage Corridor includes the 524 miles of navigable waterway of the New York State Canal System, including the Erie, Cayuga-Seneca, Oswego, and Champlain Canals, the historic alignments of these canals, and the immediately adjacent municipalities.

The federal legislation established a 27-member community-based commission. The National Park Service, the New York State Canal Corporation, and other agencies and individuals serve on the Commission and provide direction and support in the protection, promotion, and revitalization of canal communities.

OVERVIEW LOCATOR MAP

ROUTE MILEAGE

Total	Buffalo to Albany 380 miles		
Section 1	Buffalo to Rochester	92 miles	Maps 1 to 9A
Section 2	Rochester to Syracuse	113 miles	Maps 10 to 17
Section 3	Syracuse to Little Falls	85 miles	Maps 18 to 25
Section 4	Little Falls to Albany	89 miles	Maps 26 to 33A

STATE TOURISM INFORMATION

I Love NY	(800) CALL-NYS	www.iloveny.com

CANALWAY TRAIL ROUTE INFORMATION

New York State Canal Corporation	(800) 4CANAL4	www.canals.state.ny.us
Parks & Trails New York	(518) 434-1583	www.ptny.org
New York State Bike Route 5	(518) 457-7664	www.dot.state.ny.us/br5

MAJOR CANAL CORRIDOR CITIES BY POPULATION

Buffalo	292,648	Troy	49,170
Rochester	219,773	Rome	34,950
Syracuse	147,306	North Tonawanda	33,262
Albany	95,658	Lockport	22,279
Schenectady	61,821	Amsterdam	18,355
Utica	60,651		

HISTORICAL INFORMATION

Erie Canalway National Heritage Corridor	www.eriecanalway.org	(518) 237-8643
Mohawk Valley Heritage Corridor	www.mohawkvalleyheritage.com	(518) 673-1045
Western Erie Canal Heritage Corridor	www.eriecanalheritage.com	(585) 546-7029
Virtual Canal Tour	www.epodunk.com/routes/erie-canal	
Profiles of Canal Communities	www.epodunk.com	
Union College Canal Exhibit	www.eriecanal.org/UnionCollege/175th.html	
University of Rochester Department of History	www.history.rochester.edu/canal	
Historic Links, Images & Maps	www.eriecanal.org	
Canal Society of New York State	www.canalsnys.org	

TRAVEL INFORMATION

Train Lines

Amtrak	www.amtrak.com	(800) USA-RAIL
VIA Rail Canada	www.viarail.ca	(888) VIA-RAIL

Bus Lines

Trailways Transportation System	www.trailways.com	(800) 343-9999
Greyhound Lines	www.greyhound.com	(800) 229-9424

Automobile

New York State Thruway	www.thruway.state.ny.us	(800) 847-8929

Commercial Airports

Buffalo Niagara International (BUF)	www.buffaloairport.com	(716) 630-6302
Greater Rochester International (ROC)	www.rocairport.com	(585) 464-6000
Syracuse Hancock International (SYR)	www.syrairport.org	(315) 454-4330
Albany International (ALB)	www.albanyairport.com	(518) 242-2200

Regional / Local Airport Profiles www.airnav.com

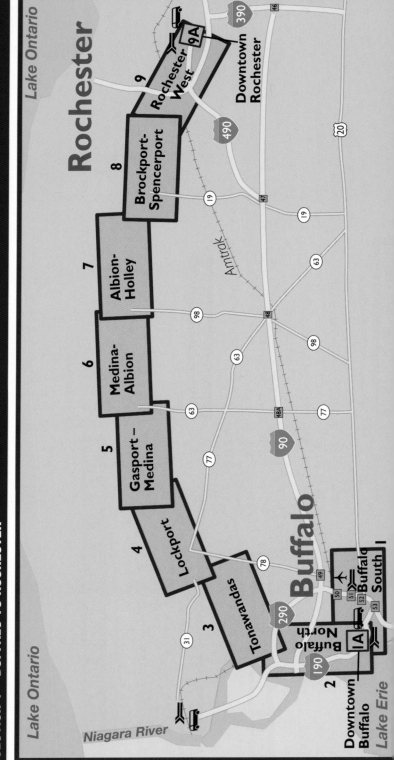

COMMUNITIES ALONG ROUTE

Erie County	Depew, Buffalo, Tonawanda
Niagara County	North Tonawanda, Lockport, Middleport,
Orleans County	Medina, Albion, Holley
Monroe County	Brockport, Spencerport, Rochester

VISITOR INFORMATION

Erie County	www.buffalocvb.org	(800) 283-3256
Niagara County	www.niagara-usa.com	(800) 338-7890
Orleans County	www.orleansny.com	(800) 724-0314
Monroe County	www.visitrochester.com	(800) 677-7282

SAFETY & SECURITY

Universal Emergency Number: 911

State Police

Troop A	Erie, Niagara, & Orleans Counties	(716) 343-2200
Troop E	Monroe County	(716) 398-3200

County Sheriff

Erie	Buffalo	(716) 858-7608
Niagara	Lockport	(716) 438-3393
Orleans	Albion	(585) 590-7000
Monroe	Rochester	(585) 428-5432

TRANSPORTATION

Amtrak Rail Stations

Niagara Falls (NFL)	27th Street & Lockport Road	(716) 285-4224
Buffalo – Downtown (BFX)	Exchange & Ellicott Streets	(716) 856-2075
Buffalo – DePew (BUF)	55 Dick Rd	(716) 683-8440
Rochester (ROC)	320 Central Ave	(585) 454-2894

Bus Stations

Transportation Center – Niagara Falls	343 4th Street	(716) 282-1331
Metropolitan Transportation Center – Buffalo	181 Ellicott Street	(716) 852-1766
Regional Transportation Center – Rochester	187 Midtown Plaza	(716) 232-5121

Urban & Regional Transit

Niagara Frontier Transportation Authority	Depew to Lockport	(716) 855-7300
	www.nfta.com	
Rochester-Genesee Transportation Authority	Brockport to Fairport	(585) 288-1700
	www.rgrta.org	

Commercial Airports

Buffalo Niagara International (BUF)	www.buffaloairport.com	(716) 630-6302
Greater Rochester International (ROC)	www.rocairport.com	(585) 464-6000

Regional / Local Airports & Airfields

Buffalo Airfield Airport (9G0)	Buffalo
Niagara Falls International Airport (IAG)	Niagara Falls
Clarence Aerodrome Airport (IAG)	Rapids
Potoczak Airport (D46)	Clarence Center
North Buffalo Suburban Airport (0G0)	Lockport
Holland International Field (85N)	Newfane
Royalton Airport (9G5)	Gasport
Pine Hills Airport (9G6)	Albion
Genesee County Airport (GVQ)	Batavia
Ledgedale Airpark Airport (7G0)	Brockport
Spencerport Airpark Airport (D91)	Spencerport

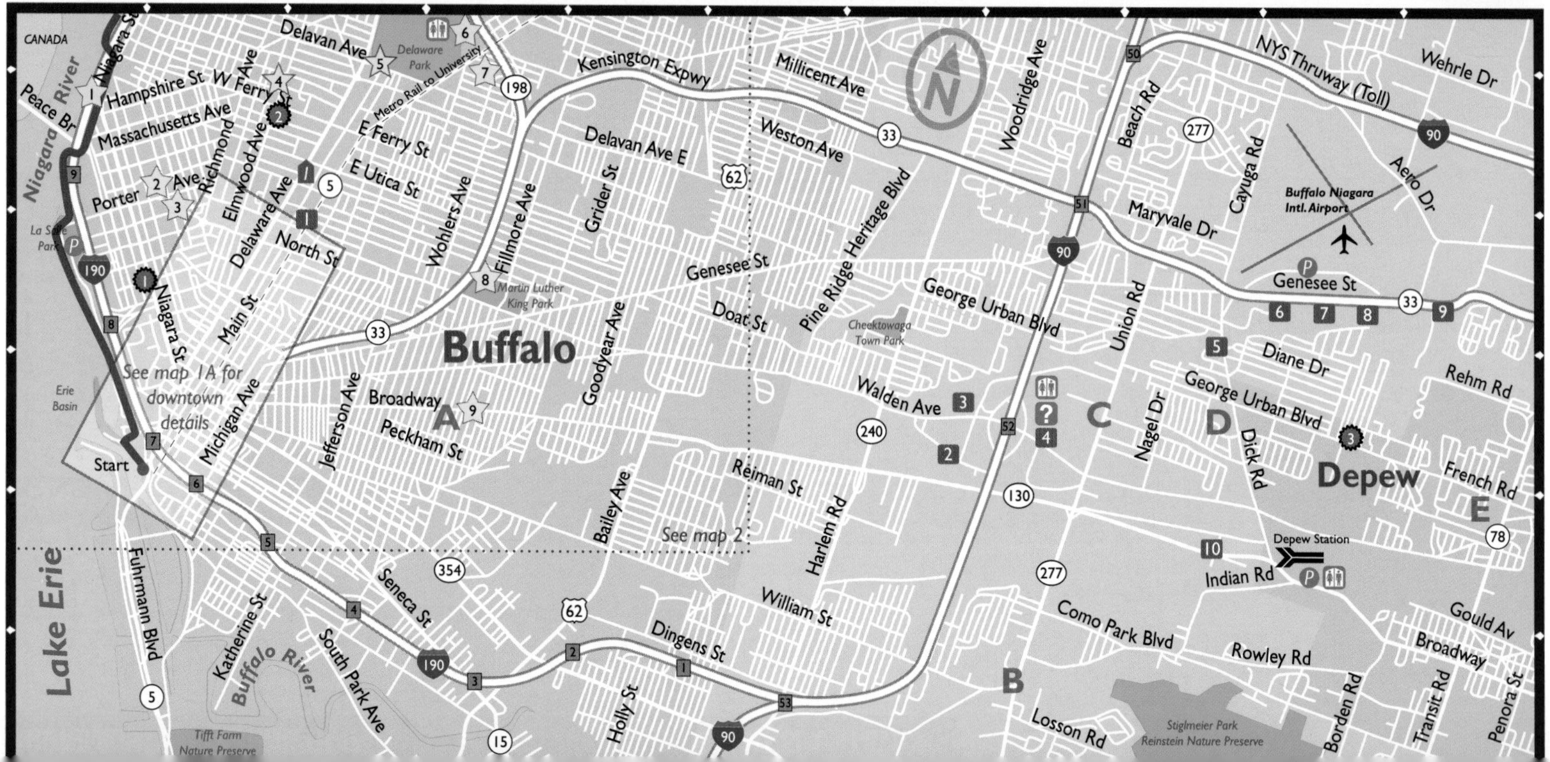

MAP 1   BUFFALO SOUTH

CANADA

Niagara River

Peace Br.

NYS Thruway (Toll)

Wehrle Dr

90

Aero Dr

9

33

Rehm Rd

French Rd

E

78

Gould Av

Broadway

Penora St

Transit Rd

Depew

3

Buffalo Niagara Intl. Airport

Genesee St

6 7 8

Diane Dr

George Urban Blvd

Dick Rd

Depew Station

Indian Rd

10

Como Park Blvd

Rowley Rd

Border Rd

Stiglmeier Park

Reinstein Nature Preserve

Losson Rd

277

B

130

52

Nagel Dr

Union Rd

C

D

5

Cayuga Rd

Maryvale Dr

Beach Rd

277

90

51

Woodridge Ave

George Urban Blvd

Walden Ave

3

2

240

Harlem Rd

William St

Dingens St

Holly St

62

2

3

90

90

33

Millicent Ave

Weston Ave

Kensington Expwy

62

Genesee St

Doat St

Cheektowaga Town Park

Pine Ridge Heritage Blvd

Rejman St

Bailey Ave

See map 2

15

Delavan Ave E

Grider St

Goodyear Ave

Buffalo

198

7

6

Delaware Park

Metro Rail to University

5

E Ferry St

E Utica St

Fillmore Ave

Wohlers Ave

Martin Luther King Park

8

Broadway

Peckham St

A

9

Jefferson Ave

354

Seneca St

190

3

4

South Park Ave

Delavan Ave

W. Ferry

Hampshire St

Massachusetts Ave

Richmond Ave

Elmwood Ave

Delaware Ave

5

1

North St

Main St

Michigan Ave

1

Niagara St

Porter

2 Ave

3

See map 1A for downtown details

6

7

Start

5

Fuhrmann Blvd

Katherine St

Buffalo River

Tifft Farm Nature Preserve

Lake Erie

Erie Basin

8

190

9

La Salle Park

Niagara St

P

THINGS TO SEE & DO

1	QRS Music Rolls	1026 Niagara Street	**(716) 885-4600**
2	D'Youville College & Kavinoky Theater	320 Porter Avenue	**(716) 881-7668**
3	Karpeles Manuscript Library Museum	453 Porter Avenue	**(716) 885-4139**
4	Ujima Theater Company	545 Elmwood Avenue	**(716) 883-0380**
5	Forest Lawn Cemetery	1411 Delaware Avenue	**(716) 885-1600**
6	Medaille College	18 Agassiz Circle	**(716) 884-0291**
7	Canisius College	2001 Main Street	**(716) 888-2525**
8	Buffalo Museum of Science & Kellogg Observatory	1020 Humboldt Parkway	**(716) 896-5200**
9	Broadway Indoor Market	999 Broadway	**(716) 893-0705**

Downtown Buffalo from the waterfront

TRAIL & TRAVEL NOTES

Historic Canal Terminus — The opening of the Erie Canal in 1825 turned the then small village of Buffalo, located at the canal's historic outlet to the Great Lakes, into the center of the shipping trade between the Midwest and Eastern United States and fueled the young nation's westward expansion.

Buffalo Waterfront — Invented here to maximize loading dock space, the remaining grain elevators that dot Buffalo's waterfront are a testament to those days when the city was the busiest grain-transfer port in the world. Take time to walk or cycle to the end of the pier at Buffalo's waterfront park to take in the view and to see the Buffalo Lighthouse, dubbed the "Chinaman's Light," because the top looks like a Chinese hat.

Chinaman's Light at Erie Basin

VISITOR INFORMATION

Visitor Center at the Galleria
Depew • (716) 686-9430
2000 Walden Avenue

SERVICE AREAS

A	$	⏱	Rx	⛟	🛏	🍴	🔧
B	$	⏱			🛏		
C	$	⏱	Rx	⛟		🛏	🔧
D	$		Rx	⛟	🛏	🍴	
E		⏱	Rx			🛏	

Richmond Ave

North St

Pearl St

Ellicott St

Elm St

Symphony Circle

Allen St

Elmwood Ave

Days Park

Virginia St

Washington St

Maryland St

St. Mary's Sq.

Edward St

Goodell St

Whitney Pl

Virginia St

Tupper St

Carolina St

Johnson Park

Franklin St

Pearl St

Ellicott St

Oak Ave

Elm St

Chippewa St

Georgia St

Elmwood Ave

Delaware Ave

Genesee St

Niagara St

Huron St

Broadway

7th St

Mohawk St

Main St

Niagara Sq.

Court St

Lafayette Sq.

190

Eagle St

Eagle St

New York State Thruway

W Genesee St

Metro Rail to University

Michigan Ave

Church St

Lakefront Blvd

Swan St

W. Seneca St

Erie Basin

Erie St

Exchange St

Exchange Street Station

190

Scott St

15

Buffalo River

Perry St

Buffalo Commercial Slip

S. Park Ave

THINGS TO SEE & DO

1	Kleinhans Music Theater / Buffalo Philharmonic	71 Symphony Circle	(716) 883-3560
2	Theodore Roosevelt Inaugural National Historic Site	641 Delaware Avenue	(716) 884-0095
3	Allentown National Preservation District	Allen Street	(716) 881-1024
4	Theater of Youth Company	203 Allen Street	(716) 884-4400
5	Studio Arena Theater	710 Main Street	(716) 856-8025
6	Alleyway Theater	1 Curtain Up Alley	(716) 852-2600
7	Buffalo Ensemble Theater at the Phoenix	95 North Johnson Park	(716) 855-2225
8	Shea's Performing Arts Center	646 Main Street	(716) 847-1410
9	Market Arcade Film & Arts Center - Dipson Theaters	638 Main Street	(716) 855-3022
10	Irish Classical Theater Company	625 Main Street	(716) 853-4282
11	CEPA Photography Gallery	617 Main Street	(716) 856-2717
12	Buffalo City Hall Observation Deck	Niagara Square	(716) 851-4200
13	Lower Lakes Marine Historical Society	66 Erie Street	(716) 849-0914
14	Buffalo Bisons Baseball (AAA)	275 Washington Street	(716) 846-2000
15	Miss Buffalo - Niagara Clipper Cruise Boat	Erie Basin Marina	(716) 856-6696
16	Naval & Military Park Museum	1 Naval Park Cove	(716) 847-1773
17	Buffalo Sabres Hockey (NHL)	1 Seymour Knox III Plaza	(716) 855-4100

TRAIL & TRAVEL NOTES

City Hall Observation Deck — Buffalo's Art Deco City Hall is the largest city hall in America. The outdoor observation deck affords a bird's eye view of the city, whose street layout is patterned after Washington, D.C.

Allentown Historic Preservation District — Allentown is a large historic preservation district listed on the National Register of Historic Places. Its Victorian buildings, restaurants, art galleries, and boutiques make it a pleasant place to spend a few hours and perhaps sample some of Buffalo's famous spicy chicken wings.

Buffalo City Hall & Niagara Square

VISITOR INFORMATION

Buffalo Convention and Visitors Bureau
(716) 852-2356
617 Main Street • www.buffalocvb.org

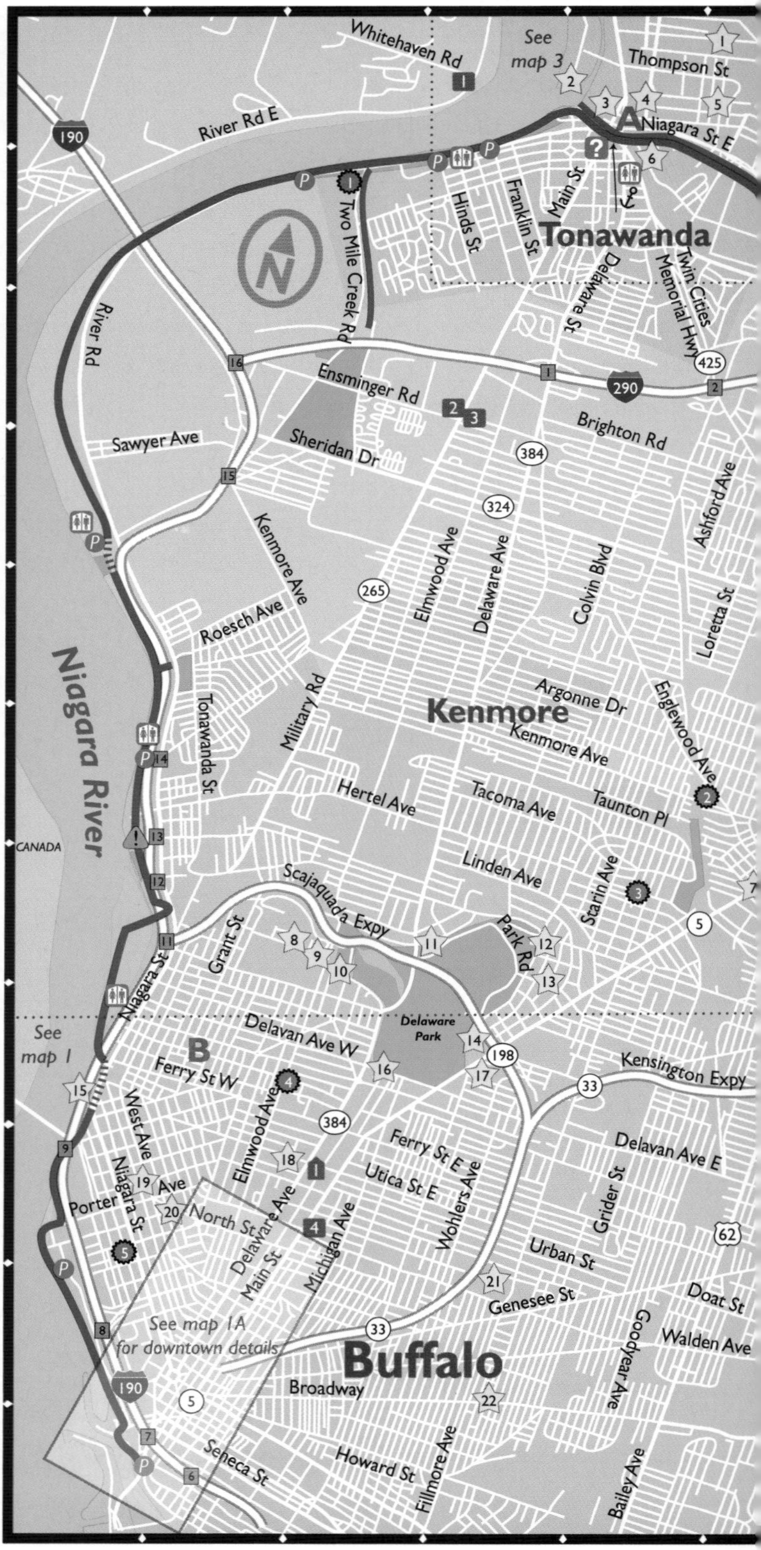
Whitehaven Rd
See map 3
Thompson St
Niagara St E
River Rd E
190
Two Mile Creek Rd
Hinds St
Franklin St
Main St
Tonawanda
Delaware St
Twin Cities Memorial Hwy
425
River Rd
Ensminger Rd
290
Brighton Rd
Sawyer Ave
Sheridan Dr
384
324
Ashford Ave
Kenmore Ave
265
Elmwood Ave
Delaware Ave
Colvin Blvd
Loretta St
Roesch Ave
Niagara River
Tonawanda St
Military Rd
Argonne Dr
Englewood Ave
Kenmore
Kenmore Ave
Hertel Ave
Tacoma Ave
Taunton Pl
CANADA
Linden Ave
Starin Ave
Scajaquada Expy
Park Rd
Grant St
Niagara St
Delavan Ave W
Delaware Park
198
Kensington Expy
See map 1
Ferry St W
West Ave
Elmwood Ave
Ferry St E
Delavan Ave E
Utica St E
Niagara St
Porter Ave
North St
Delaware Ave
Michigan Ave
Wohlers Ave
Grider St
62
Main St
Urban St
Doat St
Genesee St
Goodyear Ave
Walden Ave
See map 1A for downtown details
33
Buffalo
Broadway
Seneca St
Howard St
Fillmore Ave
Bailey Ave

THINGS TO SEE & DO

1	Herschell Carousel Factory Museum	180 Thompson Street	**(716) 693-1885**
2	Shores Waterfront Restaurant Boat Rides	2 Detroit Street	**(716) 693-6226**
3	Canal Princess Charters		**(716) 693-2752**
4	Historic Riviera Theater	67 Webster Street	**(716) 692-2413**
5	Carnegie Art Center	240 Goundry Street	**(716) 694-4400**
6	Historical Society of the Tonawandas Museum	113 Main Street	**(716) 694-7406**
7	University at Buffalo – South Campus		**(716) 645-2901**
8	Buffalo State College - Performing Arts Center	1300 Elmwood Avenue	**(716) 878-3005**
9	Burchfield-Penney Art Center	1300 Elmwood Avenue	**(716) 878-6011**
10	Albright-Knox Art Gallery	1285 Elmwood Avenue	**(716) 882-8700**
11	Buffalo & Erie County Historical Society Museum	25 Nottingham Court	**(716) 873-9644**
12	Buffalo Zoo	300 Parkside Avenue	**(716) 837-3900**
13	Darwin D. Martin House (Frank Lloyd Wright)	125 Jewett Parkway	**(716) 856-3858**
14	Medaille College	18 Agassiz Circle	**(800) 292-1582**
15	QRS Music Rolls	1026 Niagara Street	**(716) 885-4600**
16	Forest Lawn Cemetery	1411 Delaware Avenue	**(716) 885-1600**
17	Canisius College	2001 Main Street	**(716) 883-7000**
18	Theater of Youth Company	203 Allen Street	**(716) 884-4400**
19	D'Youville College & Kavinoky Theater	320 Porter Avenue	**(716) 881-7668**
20	Karpeles Manuscript Library Museum	453 Porter Avenue	**(716) 885-4139**
21	Buffalo Museum of Science & Kellogg Observatory	1020 Humboldt Parkway	**(716) 896-5200**
22	Broadway Indoor Market	999 Broadway	**(716) 893-0705**

TRAIL & TRAVEL NOTES

Buffalo as Architecture Museum — Buffalo is a veritable architecture museum, with four Frank Lloyd Wright masterpieces (including the prairie-style Darwin D. Martin House), the Louis Sullivan Guaranty Building, and a system of parks laid out by renowned landscape architect Frederick Law Olmsted.

Albright-Knox Art Gallery —The Greek Revival Albright-Knox Art Gallery has collections spanning several centuries, but is best known for its modern art, including works by Matisse, Picasso, and Pollock.

Cycling Tips — The Canalway Trail route here follows the "Riverwalk" along the Niagara River. ⚠ The trail abruptly stops at a set of stairs where the trail meets Austin Street traveling north from Squaw Island.

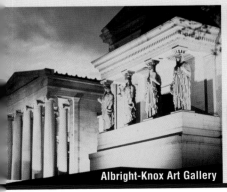

Albright-Knox Art Gallery

VISITOR INFORMATION

Chamber of Commerce of the Tonawandas
North Tonawanda • (716) 692-5120
15 Webster Street • www.the-tonawandas.com

SERVICE AREAS

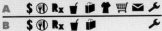

MAP 3 TONAWANDAS

26

Bear Ridge Rd

E. Canal Rd

Fisk Rd

Pendleton

263

E. Canal Rd

See map 4.

Irish Rd

Fiegle Rd

Oakwood Rd

270

Millersport Hwy

P 🛉🚻 9

Wendelville

Creek Rd N

Tonawanda Creek Rd S

Beach Ridge Rd

Killian Rd

Bear Ridge Rd

Tonawanda Creek Rd

Campbell Blvd

Schoelles Rd

270

🎣🎣 & P

Sweet Home Rd

N. French Rd

Hoffman

Shawnee Rd

425

62

Townline Rd

Tonawanda Creek Rd

Nashville

Niagara Falls Blvd

2 2

3
4

Nash Rd

5

Niagara Falls Blvd

5

🅟

Walck Rd

Sweeney St

P 🛉🚻 6

Ellicot Creek Park 7

8 9

3

2 miles

N

A
North
Tonawanda

425

Erie Ave

Robinson St

Ward Rd

Witmer Rd

429

Payne Ave

Oliver St

2

River Rd

Wheatfield St

265

384

Thompson St

B

5
7

4
8

🚻

3

Sweeney St

Niagara St

1

6

Main St

384

265

Young St

See
map 2

Creekside Dr

C

Tonawanda

Wheeler St

Niagara St

425

Niagara River

CANADA

River Rd

THINGS TO SEE & DO

#			
1	Ghostlight Theater	170 Schenck Street	(716) 743-1614
2	Herschell Carousel Factory Museum	180 Thompson Street	(716) 693-1885
3	Shores Waterfront Restaurant Boat Rides	2 Detroit Street	(716) 693-6226
4	Canal Princess Charters	24 Niagara Street	(716) 693-2752
5	Historic Riviera Theater	67 Webster Street	(716) 692-2413
6	Carnegie Art Center	240 Goundry Street	(716) 694-4400
7	Benjamin Long Homestead Museum	113 Main Street	(716) 694-7406
8	Historical Society of the Tonawandas Museum	24 East Niagara Street	(716) 694-7406
9	Amherst Museum	3755 Tonawanda Creek Road	(716) 689-1440

Entrance to Gateway Park of the Tonawandas

TRAIL & TRAVEL NOTES

Terminus of the Modern Erie Canal — Thanks to the Erie Canal, the twin cities of Tonawanda and North Tonawanda enjoyed a lumber boom in the second half of the 19th century, earning them the nickname of the "Lumber Capital of the World." Lumber, processed from raw timber from the Midwestern frontier, was one of the primary products shipped on the Erie Canal. Its low-cost availability helped fuel the rapid expansion of Eastern cities during the Industrial Era.

Herschell Carousel Factory Museum — Ride one of the two restored 20th century carousels at the Herschell Carousel Factory Museum, where you can learn how the carousel animals were carved by hand.

Cycling Tips — ⚠ When leaving the trail to join East Canal Road near Pendleton, the intersection is confusing and traffic moves quickly.

All smiles at the Herschell Carousel Factory Museum

VISITOR INFORMATION

Chamber of Commerce of the Tonawandas
North Tonawanda • (716) 692-5120
15 Webster Street • www.the-tonawandas.com

SERVICE AREAS

A	$	ⓘ	Rx	🚲	🍴	🏪	🔧
B	$	ⓘ	Rx	🚲	🍴	🏪	🔧
C	$	ⓘ	Rx	🚲	🍴	🏪	🔧
D	$	ⓘ	Rx	🚲	🍴	🏪	🔧

27

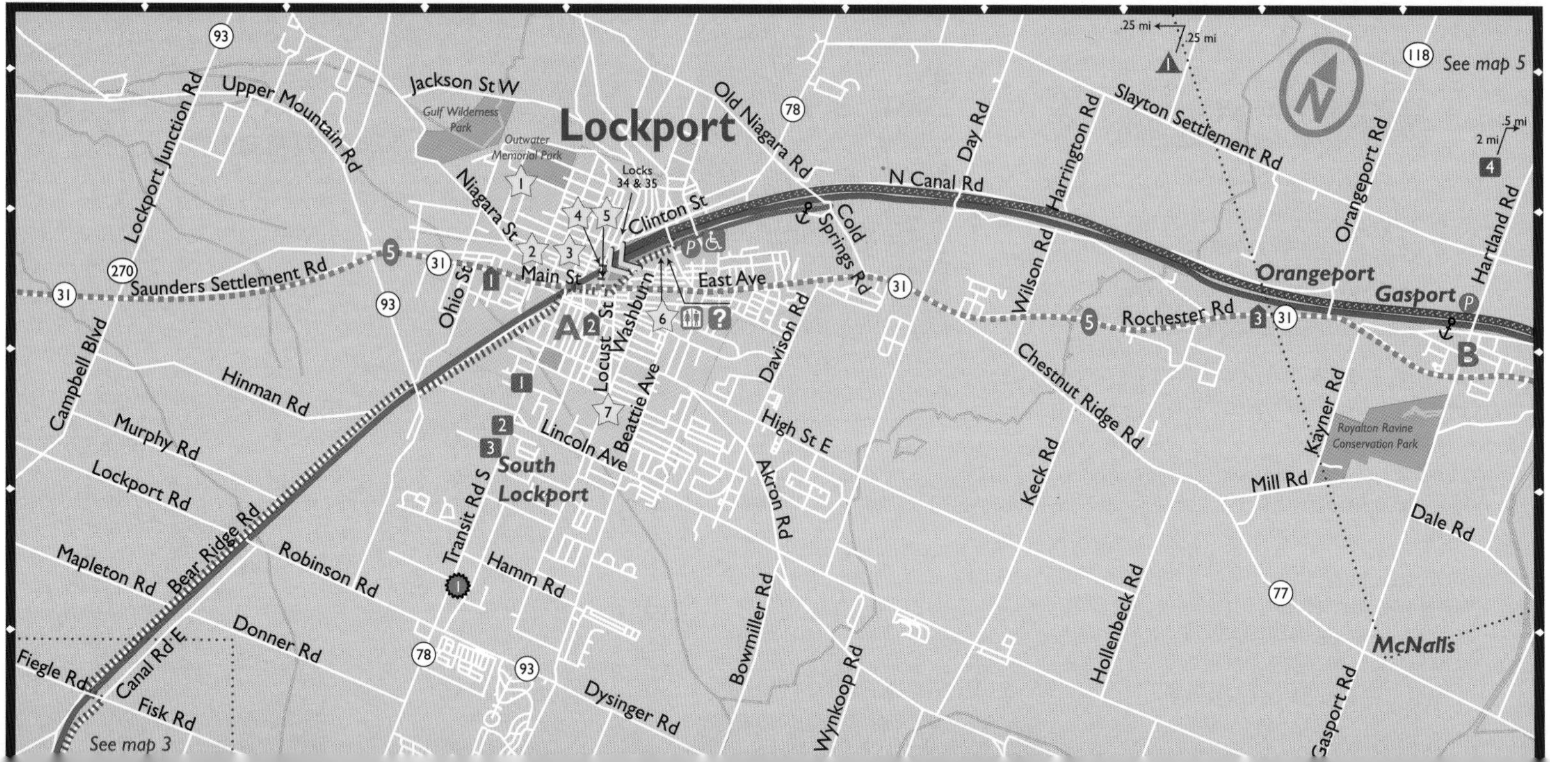

MAP 4 LOCKPORT

See map 5

Hartland Rd

Orangeport Rd

Gasport

B

Royalton Ravine
Conservation Park

Kayner Rd

Dale Rd

McNalls

Gasport Rd

118

Rochester Rd

31

Mill Rd

77

Slayton Settlement Rd

Harrington Rd

Wilson Rd

Chestnut Ridge Rd

Keck Rd

Hollenbeck Rd

Day Rd

N Canal Rd

Cold
Springs Rd

High St E

Akron Rd

Bowmiller Rd

Wynkoop Rd

Dysinger Rd

78

Old Niagara Rd

Davison Rd

East Ave

Lockport

Locks
34 & 35

Clinton St

Washburn St

Locust St

Beattie Ave

Lincoln Ave

South
Lockport

Hamm Rd

Jackson St W

Gulf Wilderness
Park

Outwater
Memorial Park

Niagara St

Main St

Ohio St

Transit Rd S

93

78

Upper Mountain Rd

93

Lockport Junction Rd

270

Saunders Settlement Rd

31

93

Hinman Rd

Murphy Rd

Lockport Rd

Bear Ridge Rd

Robinson Rd

Donner Rd

Campbell Blvd

Mapleton Rd

Fiegle Rd

Canal Rd E

Fisk Rd

See map 3

.25 mi

.25 mi

2 mi

5 mi

THINGS TO SEE & DO

1	Speedway Park	400 Corinthia Street	**(716) 772-7591**
2	Niagara County Historical Society Museum	215 Niagara Street	**(716) 434-7433**
3	Colonel William Bond House	143 Ontario Street	**(716) 434-7433**
4	New York State Erie Canal Museum (Lock 34/35)	80 Richmond Avenue	**(716) 434-3140**
5	Lockport Caves And Underground Boat Ride	21 Main Street	**(716) 438-0174**
6	Lockport Locks & Erie Canal Heritage Center	210 Market Street	**(716) 433-6155**
7	Kenan Center	433 Locust Street	**(716) 433-2617**

Modern Lockport Locks

TRAIL & TRAVEL NOTES

Niagara Escarpment — Lockport derives its name from the locks that were built to partially overcome the 70-foot difference in elevation as the canal crosses the Niagara Escarpment, a massive geological formation of sedimentary rock cliffs running in a northern arc around Lakes Huron and Michigan to Wisconsin. Niagara Falls is a result of the water from Lake Erie spilling over the Escarpment on its way to Lake Ontario.

Lockport Locks — In Lockport, one of two original sets of five-step locks built in 1825 stands alongside a modern working double canal lock, making for a great comparison of two centuries of canal engineering. Commercial boat rides enable visitors to "lock through" these engineering marvels.

Cycling Tips — The longest unbroken stretch of the Canalway Trail Route that is off-road begins in Lockport and continues 85 miles to Palmyra. Niagara Falls is less than 15 miles from Lockport on Bike Route 5.

3792. *The Locks, Lockport, N. Y.*
Historic "Flight of Five" Locks

VISITOR INFORMATION

Market Street Art Center
Lockport • (716) 478-0083
247 Market Street • www.marketstreetstudios.com

SERVICE AREAS

A $ ⑩ Rx ✗ 🏠 🍴 🔧
🛏 ⛽ 🔨

B $ ⑩
🛏 ⛽

29

MAP 5 GASPORT – MEDINA

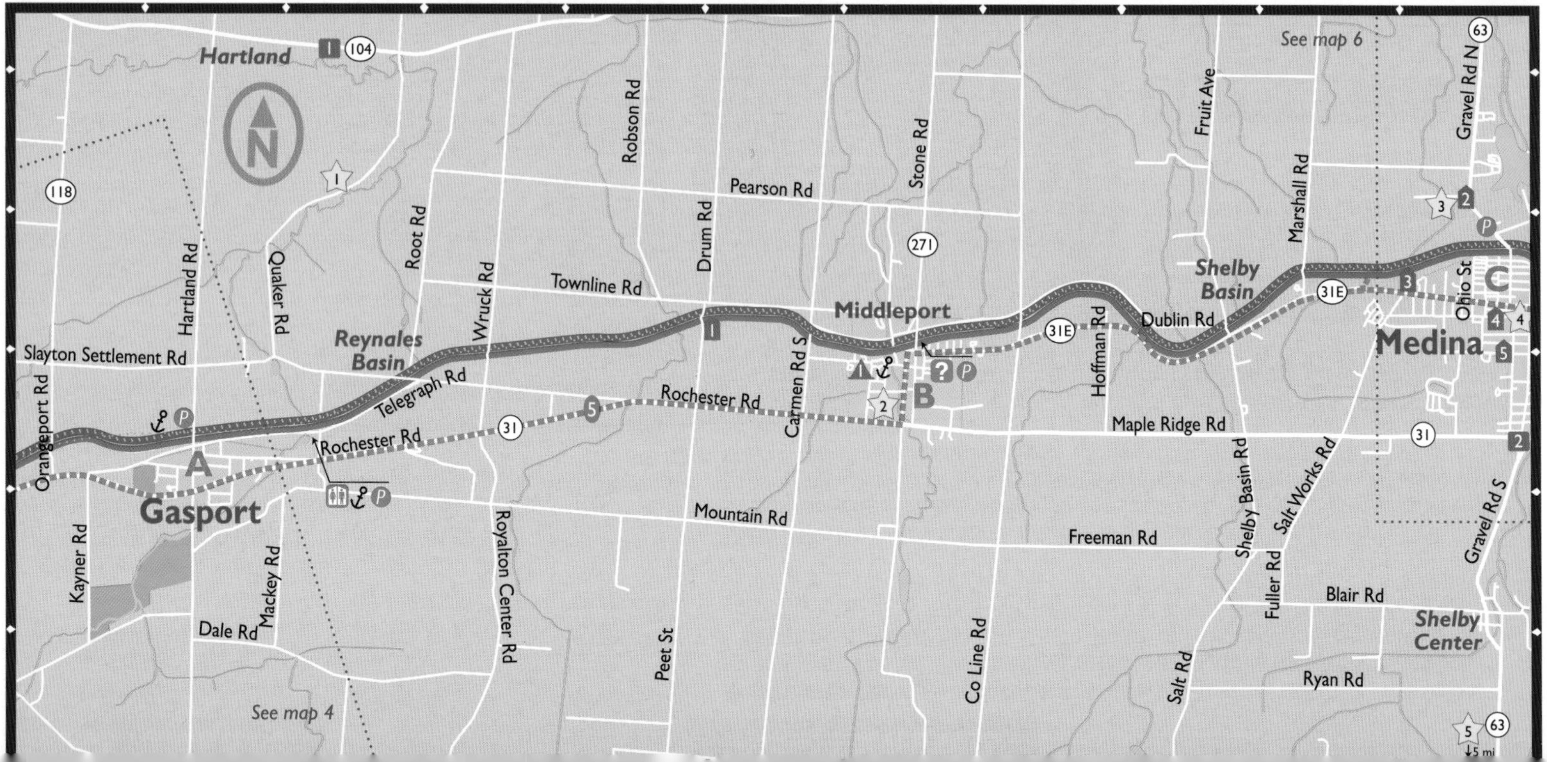

Gravel Rd N (63)

Ohio St

C

Medina

Gravel Rd S

Shelby Center

(63)

5 mi

(31)

Blair Rd

Ryan Rd

See map 6

Marshall Rd

31E

Salt Works Rd

Fuller Rd

Shelby Basin Rd

Salt Rd

Fruit Ave

Shelby Basin

Dublin Rd

Maple Ridge Rd

Hoffman Rd

31E

Freeman Rd

Co Line Rd

Stone Rd

(271)

Middleport

B

Carmen Rd S

Pearson Rd

Drum Rd

Rochester Rd

Mountain Rd

Peet St

Robson Rd

Townline Rd

1

Wruck Rd

(31)

Royalton Center Rd

Root Rd

Reynales Basin

Telegraph Rd

Rochester Rd

Quaker Rd

Hartland

(104)

1

Hartland Rd

A

Gasport

Mackey Rd

Dale Rd

See map 4

Slayton Settlement Rd

Orangeport Rd

Kayner Rd

(118)

N

THINGS TO SEE & DO

1. Becker Farms — 3760 Quaker Road — (585) 772-2211
2. Shops At Tea Hollow — 106 Telegraph Road — (716) 735-7164
3. Heritage Barn & Hoedown Tour at Stone Farm — 255 Route 63N — (585) 789-9238
4. Medina Railroad Museum — 530 West Avenue — (585) 798-6106
5. Iroquois National Wildlife Refuge — 1101 Casey Road — (585) 948-5445

Historic image of loading apple barrels in Medina

A present-day tribute to Medina's apple-producing heritage

TRAIL & TRAVEL NOTES

Rich Farmland — The importance of agriculture to New York State's economy is evident along the next 50-mile stretch of Canalway Trail, where the moderate climate created by nearby Lake Ontario provides ideal conditions for growing fruit, especially apples and grapes.

Medina Sandstone — Medina is notable for the local abundance of a reddish-brown sedimentary rock known as Medina Sandstone. The hard sandstone was shipped, mostly via the Erie Canal, to cities as far away as London. Medina and the surrounding communities exhibit many fine examples of sandstone architecture.

"Port" Towns — The western half of the Erie Canal traversed areas that were virtual wildernesses at the turn of the 19th century. Once the Canal was built, "port" towns quickly sprang up at regular intervals.

Attractive brick home with Medina Sandstone details

VISITOR INFORMATION

Middleport Village Hall
Middleport • (716) 735-3303
24 Main Street • www.middleport-ny.com

SERVICE AREAS

A	$		
B	$		
C	$	Rx	

31

MAP 6   MEDINA – ALBION

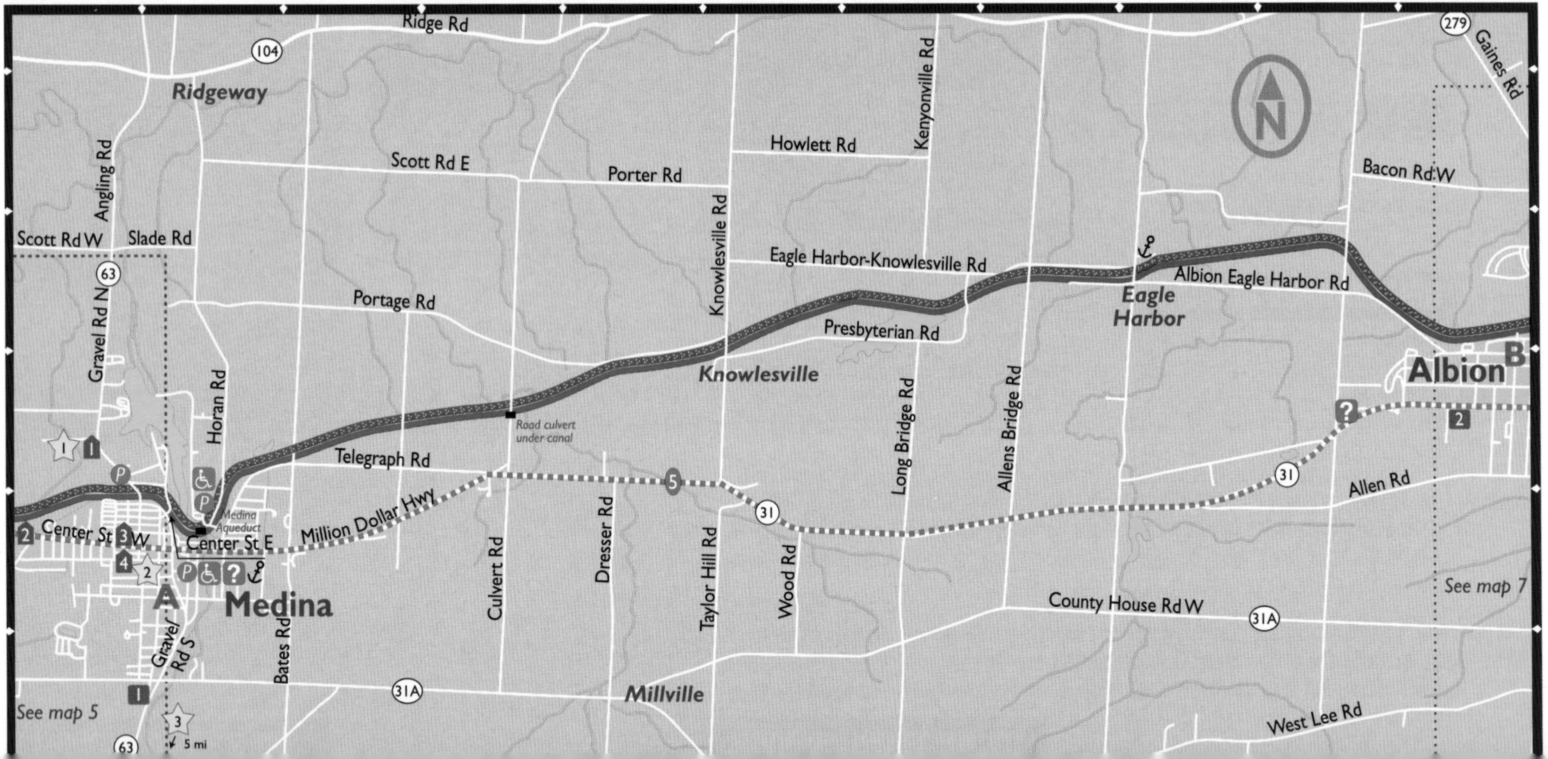

Gaines Rd (279)

Bacon Rd W

Albion **B**

Albion Eagle Harbor Rd

Eagle Harbor

Allen Rd

(31)

(31A)

County House Rd W

West Lee Rd

See map 7

Allens Bridge Rd

Kenyonville Rd

Howlett Rd

Eagle Harbor-Knowlesville Rd

Presbyterian Rd

Long Bridge Rd

Wood Rd

(31)

Porter Rd

Knowlesville Rd

Knowlesville

Taylor Hill Rd

Dresser Rd

(5)

Millville

Scott Rd E

Ridge Rd

Portage Rd

Road culvert under canal

Culvert Rd

(31A)

Telegraph Rd

Bates Rd

Million Dollar Hwy

Medina Aqueduct

Horan Rd

Ridgeway (104)

Slade Rd

Angling Rd

Scott Rd W

Gravel Rd N (63)

Center St W

Center St E

Center St

Medina

A

Gravel Rd S

(63)

See map 5

1 5 mi

3

N

THINGS TO SEE & DO

1 Heritage Barn & Hoedown at Medina Stone Farm	255 Route 63N	**(585) 789-9238**
2 Medina Railroad Museum	530 West Avenue	**(585) 798-6106**
3 Iroquois National Wildlife Refuge	1101 Casey Road	**(585) 948-5445**

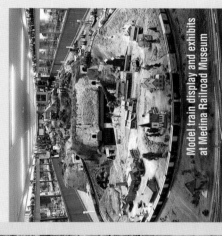

Boat passing over only road to go under canal

TRAIL & TRAVEL NOTES

A Glacial Lakeshore — This level section of the Erie Canal, known as the "upper long level," follows the edge of a prehistoric glacial lake for over 70 miles from Lockport to just east of Rochester.

Only Road Under Erie Canal — About two miles east of Medina, the Erie Canal runs over Culvert Road – the only place where a road passes under the canal. Listed in Ripley's *Believe It or Not*, it's a strange feeling indeed to stand under the Erie Canal and have canal water drip down your neck.

Cycling Tips — A designated bicycle route runs roughly parallel to the canal along the shore of Lake Ontario located about 10 miles to the north. A guidebook is available from the New York State Seaway Trail, a National Scenic Byway (1-800-Seaway).

Model train display and exhibits at Medina Railroad Museum

VISITOR INFORMATION

Orleans County Chamber of Commerce
Medina • (585) 798-4287
433 Main Street • www.orleanschamber.com

Orleans County Tourism Agency
Albion • (585) 589-3198
14016 Route 31 W • www.orleansny.com

SERVICE AREAS

A

B

MAP 7   ALBION – HOLLEY

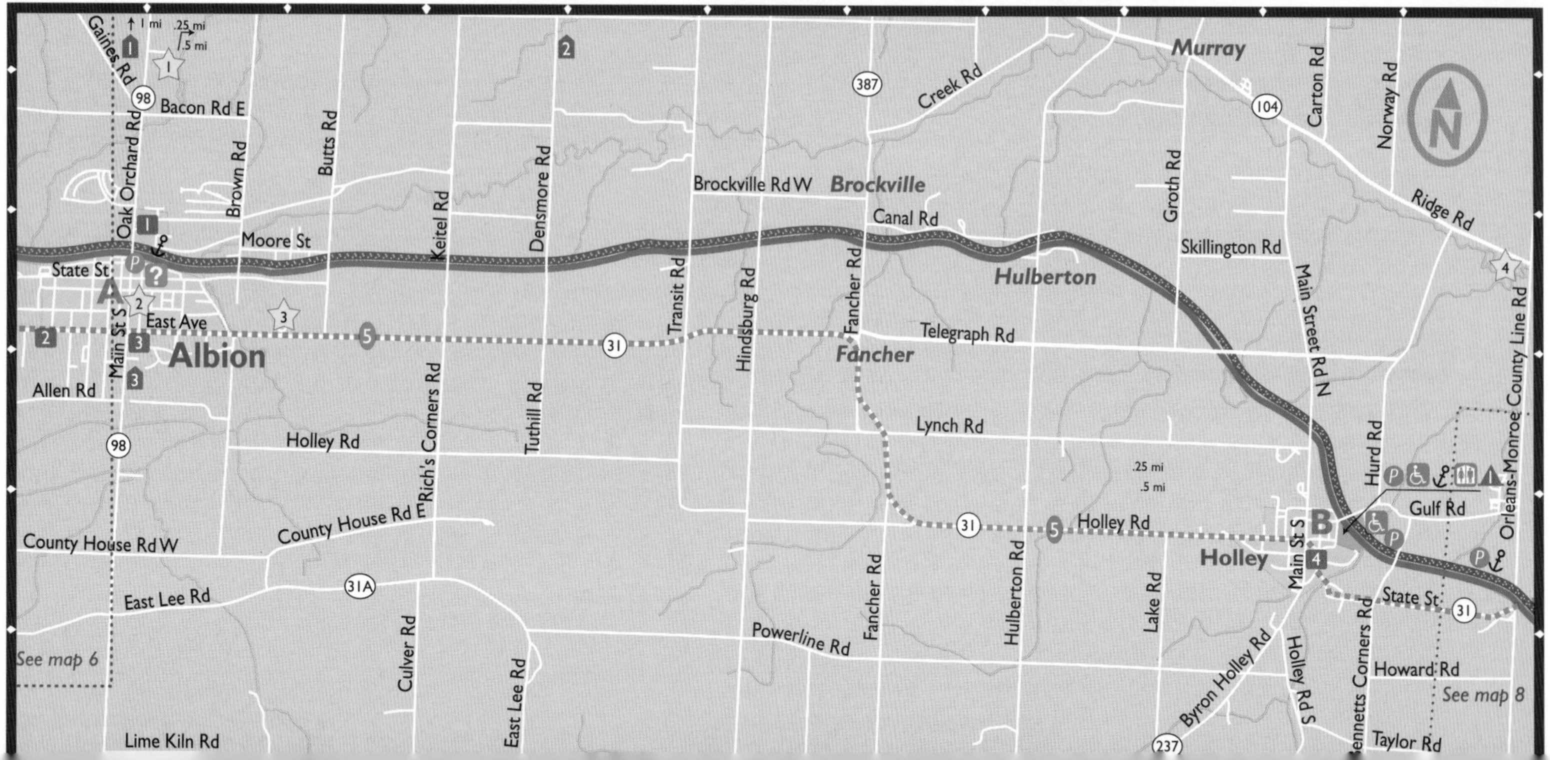

34

Norway Rd

Ridge Rd

Orleans-Monroe County Line Rd

See map 8

Carton Rd

Murray

104

Main Street Rd N

Gulf Rd

Hurd Rd

State St

Howard Rd

Taylor Rd

Skillington Rd

31

Kennetts Corners Rd

Groth Rd

B

Main St S

Holley Rd S

Holley

Hulberton

Byron Holley Rd

Creek Rd

Canal Rd

Lake Rd

237

387

Brockville

Telegraph Rd

.25 mi
.5 mi

Holley Rd

Brockville Rd W

Fancher

Lynch Rd

31

Hulberton Rd

Fancher Rd

Hindsburg Rd

Fancher Rd

Powerline Rd

Transit Rd

2

Densmore Rd

Tuthill Rd

31

East Lee Rd

Keitel Rd

Rich's Corners Rd

Culver Rd

Butts Rd

Holley Rd

County House Rd E

31A

Bacon Rd E

Moore St

3

Brown Rd

Albion

East Lee Rd

Lime Kiln Rd

1 mi
.25 mi
.5 mi

1

98

Gaines Rd

Oak Orchard Rd

State St

P

2

East Ave

A

Main St S

98

Allen Rd

County House Rd E

See map 6

County House Rd W

2

N

THINGS TO SEE & DO

1	Cobblestone Society Museum	14393 Ridge Road West	(585) 589-9013
2	Courthouse Square Historic District	Route 98 and Park Avenue	(585) 589-4174
3	Mount Albion Cemetery	Route 31E	(585) 589-4174
4	Hurd Orchards	West Ridge Road	(585) 638-8838

Cobblestone wall detail

Cobblestone Society Museum

TRAIL & TRAVEL NOTES

Cobblestone Era — Cobblestone masonry flourished during the peak of the canal's commercial use between 1825 and 1860, leaving a legacy of more than 1,000 cobblestone buildings within a 75-mile radius of Rochester. As farmers cleared fields to plant grain that could now easily be shipped out on the canal, the unearthed cobblestones were used as an inexpensive building material. Many fine cobblestone buildings can be seen in the area, especially along Ridge Road.

Courthouse Square Historic District — Albion's 1858 silver-domed Greek Revival courthouse is the centerpiece of the Courthouse Square Historic District, listed in the National and State Registers of Historic Places.

Cycling Tips — Holley has a nice biker/hiker/boater facility that includes one of the new overnight camping facilities being established along the trail by the NYS Canal Corporation.

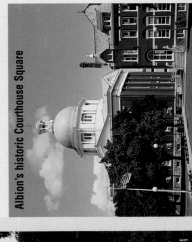

Albion's historic Courthouse Square

VISITOR INFORMATION

Orleans County Chamber of Commerce
Albion • (585) 589-7727
121 N Main Street, Suite 110
www.orleanschamber.com

SERVICE AREAS

A $ Rx 🛏 🎁 🍴 🔧 ⚒
B $ ⛽ 🎣

MAP 8 BROCKPORT – SPENCERPORT

Union St N — 259

West Ave

Spencerport B

Nichols St

Union St S — 259

Canal Rd

Trimmer Rd

Vroom Rd

531

Pine Hill Rd

31

Colby St

Chambers St

Lyell St

Hinkleyville Rd

Adams Basin

Brockport Spencerport Rd

Washington St

36

5

Clarkson Parma Town Line Rd

Ogden Parma Townline Rd

Gallup Rd

Hubbell Rd

Northampton Park

Gordon Rd

Campbell Rd

104

Ridge Rd

East Ave

260

Sweden Walker Rd

Salmon Creek Rd

19

Clarkson

Canal Rd E

Owens Rd

31

Shumway Rd

Colby St

Swamp Rd

Sweden Center

Lake Rd

State St

A

Lake Rd

White Rd

19

2

Brockport

Holley St

Fourth Section Rd

1

Redman Rd

West Ave

Canal Rd W

31

Redman Rd

Sweden Rd W

4

Edmunds Rd

31

31a

Monroe Orleans County Line Rd

See map 5

See map 7

See map 7

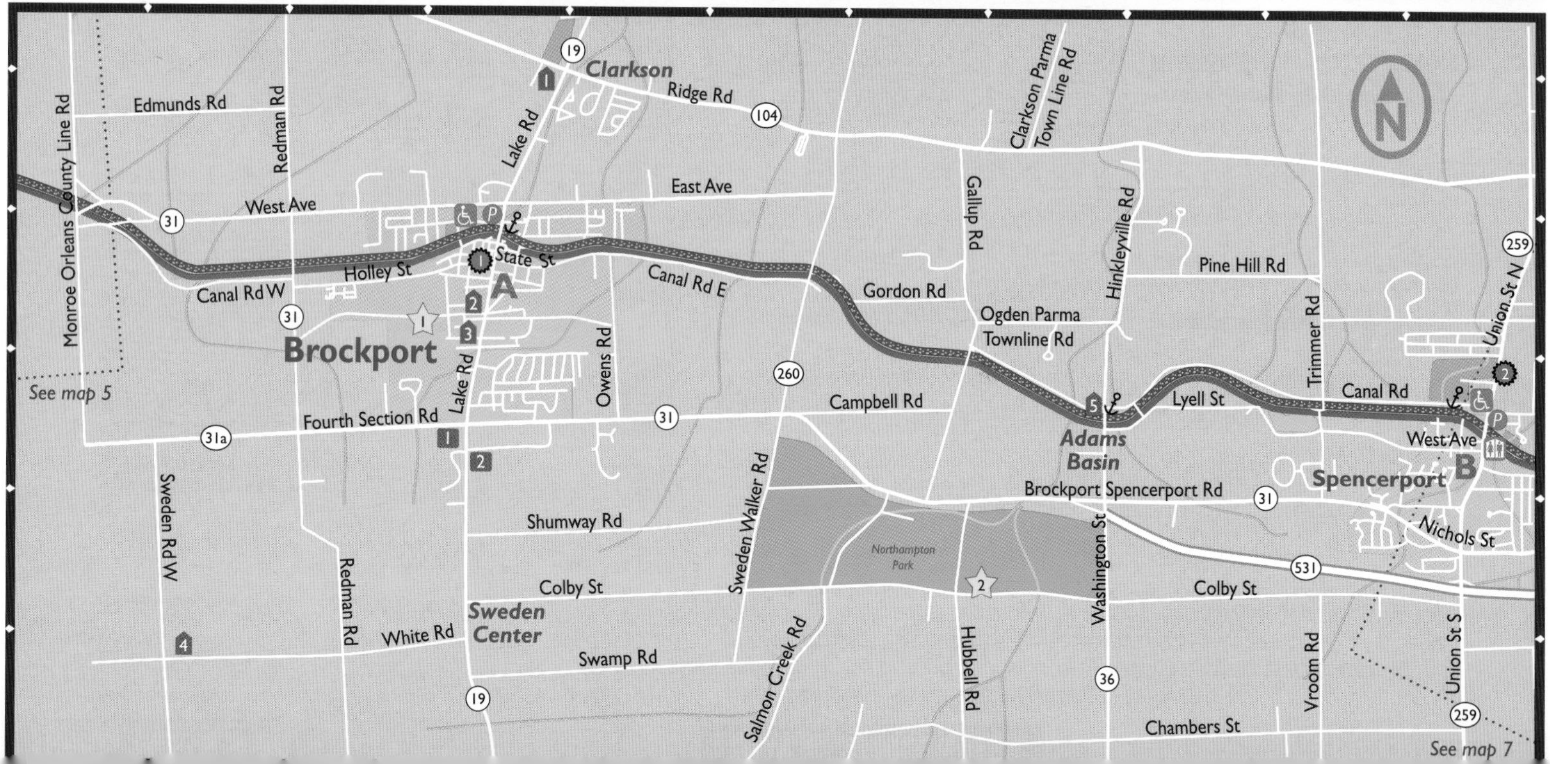

THINGS TO SEE & DO

1	State University of New York at Brockport	350 New Campus Drive	(585) 395-2751
2	Springdale Farms	696 Colby Street	(585) 352-5320

Spencerport waterfront & lift bridge

TRAIL & TRAVEL NOTES

Amber Waves of Grain — The Erie Canal reduced the cost of shipping wheat from Western New York and the Midwest to New York City by 80 to 90 percent. In the mid 19th century, one-quarter of the grain grown in the U.S. traveled to market via the canal. Although by 1847 more of the wheat shipped on the Erie Canal originated from other states, New York continued to prosper from the canal by shifting to higher value crops and handling grain produced elsewhere.

Canal "Vintage" Communities — Since construction of the original four-foot-deep "Clinton's Ditch" in 1825, the Erie Canal has gone through several route changes. However, in Western New York (unlike in Central and Eastern New York) the present-day canal still follows the alignment of the earliest canal. This means that the towns and villages along this part of the route are of original canal "vintage."

Spencerport canalside gazebo

SERVICE AREAS

A	$	🏠	🚻	🛏	🍴	⛽	🔧
B	$	💊	🚻	🛏	🍴	🛒	

37

MAP 9 ROCHESTER WEST

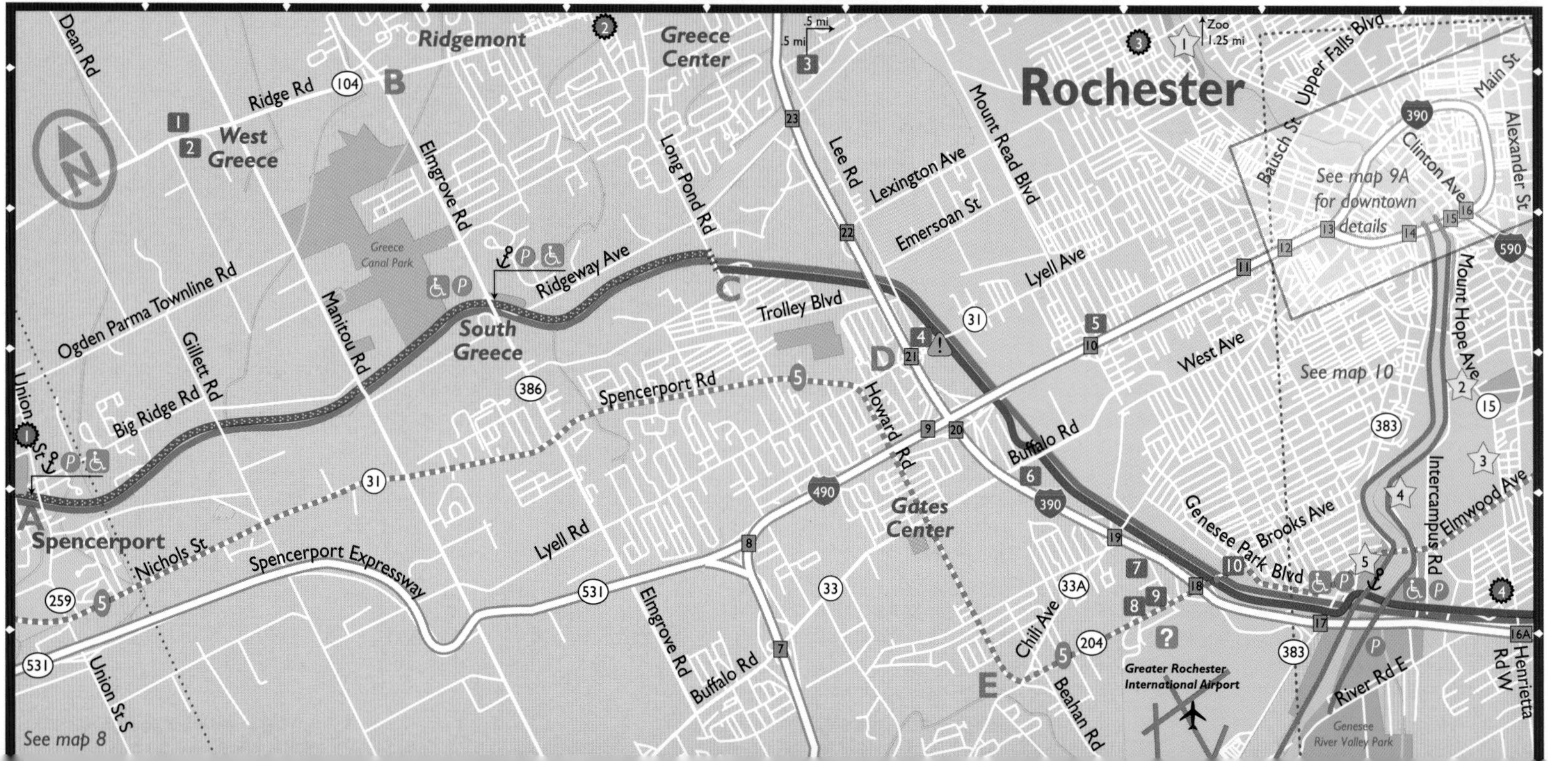

Henrietta
Rd W

Alexander St

Main St

Mount Hope Ave

590

15

3

Elmwood Ave

Clinton Ave

390

See map 9A
for downtown
details

Intercampus Rd

2

4

383

16

15

14

13

12

Bausch St

Upper Falls Blvd

See map 10

383

5

River Rd E

Genesee River Valley Park

Zoo
.25 mi

Rochester

West Ave

Genesee Park Blvd

Brooks Ave

12

Greater Rochester
International Airport

River Rd W

Mount Read Blvd

Lyell Ave

5

Buffalo Rd

5

18

19

383

7

8

9

204

Beahan Rd

Chili Ave

Lexington Ave

Emerson St

Lee Rd

31

Buffalo Rd

6

390

33A

5

E

5 mi
5 mi

23

Long Pond Rd

Trolley Blvd

22

Howard Rd

9

20

21

4

D

Gates
Center

490

33

Ridgeway Ave

Greece
Center

Elmgrove Rd

Greece Canal Park

South
Greece

Spencerport Rd

5

C

7

8

Buffalo Rd

Elmgrove Rd

Lyell Rd

531

Ridgemont

2

104

Ridge Rd

West
Greece

Dean Rd

Elmgrove Rd

Manitou Rd

386

B

31

Spencerport Expressway

Ogden Parma Townline Rd

Gillett Rd

Big Ridge Rd

Nichols St

Spencerport

Union St

259

531

5

Union St S

A

See map 8

N

THINGS TO SEE & DO

1	Seneca Park Zoo	2222 St Paul Street	(585) 336-7200
2	Ellwanger Garden	625 Mount Hope Avenue	(585) 546-7029
3	Mount Hope Cemetery	1133 Mount Hope Avenue	(585) 342-1516
4	University of Rochester	Intercampus Drive	(585) 275-2121
5	Canoe & Kayak Rentals	Genesee Valley Park Boathouse	(585) 428-7889

High Falls

TRAIL & TRAVEL NOTES

Meeting of the Trails — In Genesee Valley Park, the Erie Canalway Trail meets up with two other trails, the Genesee Riverway Trail and the Genesee Valley Greenway. The 13-mile Genesee Riverway Trail provides a mostly off-road route into downtown Rochester and north to Lake Ontario. The Genesee Valley Greenway runs southward, eventually to extend 90 miles almost to the Pennsylvania border. Currently, 52 miles of the Greenway trail are complete. About 35 miles south of Rochester, the Greenway passes through Letchworth State Park, often called the Grand Canyon of the East because of its 600-foot-deep gorge. For Greenway information, contact Friends of the Genesee Valley Greenway (www.fogvg.org / 585-658-2569).

Cycling Tips — ⚠ Tree roots have pushed up the surface of the paved Canalway Trail west of Rochester. Beware of very large bumps. The Lyell Avenue crossing is very busy with poor site lines and visibility.

Junction of the Erie & Genesee Trails

VISITOR INFORMATION

Information Kiosk
Rochester Airport Terminal • (585) 464-6801
1200 Brooks Avenue

SERVICE AREAS

A	$	⏚	Rx	🍴	🛏	🏪	⛽	🔧
B	$	⏚	Rx	🍴	🛏	🏪	⛽	🔧
C	$	⏚						🔧
D	$	⏚	Rx	🍴	🛏	🏪		🔧
E	$	⏚	Rx	🍴	🛏	🏪	⛽	🔧

MAP 9A   DOWNTOWN ROCHESTER

Genesee River

Jones Sq. Park

Smith St

Lake Ave

Bausch St

St Paul St

Ward St

Central Ave

Inner Loop

Joseph Ave

Harrison St

North St

Falls St

Frankfort St

N Plymouth Ave

Verona St

Brown Sq Park

Oak St

Broad St

Walnut St

Campbell St

Brown St

Allen St

King St

Madison

Jefferson Ave

W Main St

Troup St

Ford St

Atkinson St

Plymouth Ave

W Broad St

W Broad St

W Main St

State St

Morrie Silver Way

Browns Race

Genesee Crossroads Park

Andrews St

St Paul St

N Clinton Ave

N Pleasant St

Scio St

E Main St

University Ave

Lyndhurst St

Weld St

Woodward St

Ontario St

Lewis St

N Union St

Railroad St

E Main St

Circle St

College Ave

Prince St

Alexander St

Anderson Ave

Atlantic Ave

University Ave

Merriman St

Upton Pk

N Goodman St

East Ave

Park St

Meigs St

Rowley St

S Goodman St

Monroe Ave

Edgerton St

Barrington St

Westminster Rd

Dartmouth St

Vick Park B

Vick Park A

Rutgers St

Oxford St

Harvard St

E Broad St

Chestnut St

Broadway

East Ave

Inner Loop

S Union St

S Clinton Ave

Woodbury Blvd

Court St

Regional Transportation Center

Genesee Aqueduct

Genesee Gateway Park

Jefferson Ave

Amtrak
Rochester

Washington Sq

31

96

490

490

490

490

96

33

31

12

15

383

15

THINGS TO SEE & DO

#			
1	Susan B. Anthony House	17 Madison Street	(585) 235-6124
2	Rochester Rhino Soccer	333 N Plymoth Avenue	(585) 454-5425
3	Rochester Red Wings Baseball (AAA)	1 Morrie Silver Way	(585) 454-1001
4	High Falls Heritage Area & Entertainment District	60 Browns Race	(716) 325-2030
5	Rochester City Hall	30 Church Street	(585) 428-7000
6	Blue Cross Arena & Rochester Americans Hockey	1 War Memorial Square	(585) 758-5330
7	Campbell-Whittlesey Museum / Landmark Society of Western NY	123 South Fitzhugh Street	(585) 546-7029
8	Sam Patch Tour Boat	250 Exchange Boulevard	(585) 262-5661
9	Downstairs Cabaret Theater	20 Windsor Street	(585) 325-4370
10	Eastman School of Music Theater	26 Gibbs Street	(585) 274-1100
11	Rochester Philharmonic Orchestra	108 East Avenue	(585) 454-2100
12	Blackfriars Theater	28 Lawn Street	(585) 454-1260
13	Geva Theater	75 Woodbury Boulevard	(585) 232-4382
14	Strong Museum	1 Manhattan Square	(585) 263-2700
15	Memorial Art Gallery	500 University Avenue	(585) 473-7720
16	Woodside Mansion	485 East Avenue	(585) 271-2705
17	Rochester Museum, Science Center & Planetarium	657 East Avenue	(716) 271-4320
18	George Eastman House Museum of Photography & Film	900 East Avenue	(585) 271-3361
19	Rochester Chamber Orchestra	950 East Avenue	(716) 473-6711

TRAIL & TRAVEL NOTES

Erie Canal – "Mother of Cities" — Rochester was one of several 'boom towns' created by the Erie Canal. The combination of surrounding rich farmland, availability of waterpower, and inexpensive canal transportation turned the city into the 19th century flour capital of the world.

Genesee River Aqueduct — The Genesee Aqueduct, which once brought Erie Canal traffic over the Genesee River, today carries Broad Street, a major commercial thoroughfare.

Cycling Tips — ⚠ The Genesee Riverway Trail shifts from off-road to city streets for several blocks through downtown Rochester, starting at the Court Street Bridge sidewalk. Look for trail markers indicating the route to High Falls and Seneca Park.

Historic aqueduct now carries Broad Street

VISITOR INFORMATION

The Center At High Falls
(585) 325-2030
60 Browns Race • www.centerathighfalls.org

Downtown Guides
(585) 232-3420
120 E Main Street
www.rochesterdowntown.com/about/about_guides.html

Greater Rochester Visitor Association
(585) 546-3070
45 East Avenue • www.visitrochester.com

Arts and Cultural Association of Greater Rochester
(585) 473-4000
277 North Goodman Street • www.artsrochester.org

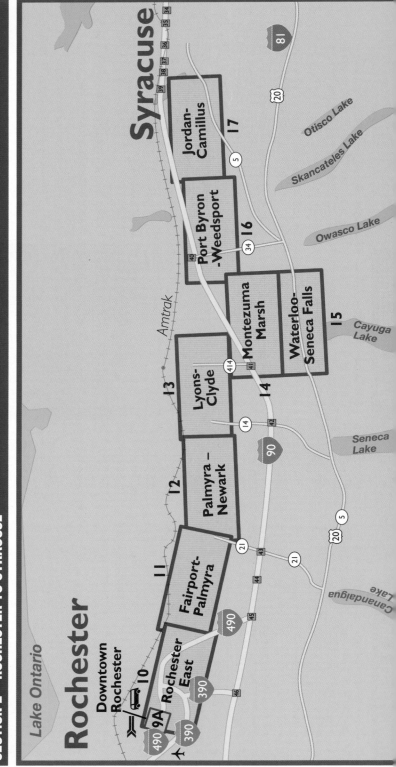

COMMUNITIES ALONG ROUTE

Monroe County	Rochester, Pittsford, Fairport
Wayne County	Macedon, Palmyra, Newark, Lyons, Clyde
Seneca County	Waterloo, Seneca Falls
Cayuga County	Port Byron, Weedsport
Onondaga County	Jordan, Camillus

VISITOR INFORMATION

Monroe County	www.visitrochester.com	(800) 677-7282
Wayne County	www.tourism.co.wayne.ny.us	(800) 527-6510
Ontario County	www.visitfingerlakes.com	(877) 386-4669
Seneca County	www.co.seneca.ny.us	(800) 732-1848
Cayuga County	www.tourcayuga.com	(800) 499-9615
Onondaga County	www.visitsyracuse.org	(800) 234-4797

SAFETY & SECURITY

Universal Emergency Number: 911

State Police

Troop E	Monroe, Wayne, Seneca, & Cayuga Counties	(716) 398-3200
Troop D	Onondaga County	(315) 366-6000

County Sheriff

Monroe	Rochester	(585) 428-5432
Wayne	Lyons	(315) 946-9711
Seneca	Waterloo	(315) 539-9241
Cayuga	Auburn	(315) 258-9111
Onondaga	Syracuse	(315) 435-3044

TRANSPORTATION

Amtrak Rail Stations

Rochester (ROC)	320 Central Avenue	(585) 454-2894
Syracuse (SYR)	131 P&C Parkway	(315) 477-1152

Bus Stations

Regional Transportation Center – Rochester	187 Midtown Plaza	(716) 232-5121
Regional Transportation Center – Syracuse	131 P&C Parkway	(315) 477-1152

Urban & Regional Transit

Rochester-Genesee Transportation Authority	Brockport to Fairport www.rgrta.org	(585) 288-1700
Central New York Transportation Authority	Port Byron to Fayetteville www.centro.org	(315) 442-3400

Fast Ferry: Rochester-Toronto

Canadian American Transportation System	www.catsfastferry.com	(877) 825-3774/ (585) 663-0790

Commercial Airports

Greater Rochester International (ROC)	www.rocairport.com	(585) 464-6000
Syracuse Hancock International (SYR)	www.syrairport.org	(315) 454-4330

Regional / Local Airports & Airfields

Canandaigua Airport (D38)	Canandaigua
Hopewell Airpark (D43)	Canandaigua
Farnsworths Air Strip Airport (8B4)	North Rose
Airtrek Airport (D93)	Waterloo
Finger Lakes Regional Airport (0G7)	Seneca Falls
Whitfords Airport (B16)	Weedsport
Skaneateles Aerodrome Airport (6B9)	Skaneateles
Camillus Airport (NY2)	Camillus
Airlane Enterprises Airport (1H1)	Clay
Michael Airfield Airport (1G6)	Cicero

43

MAP 10 ROCHESTER EAST

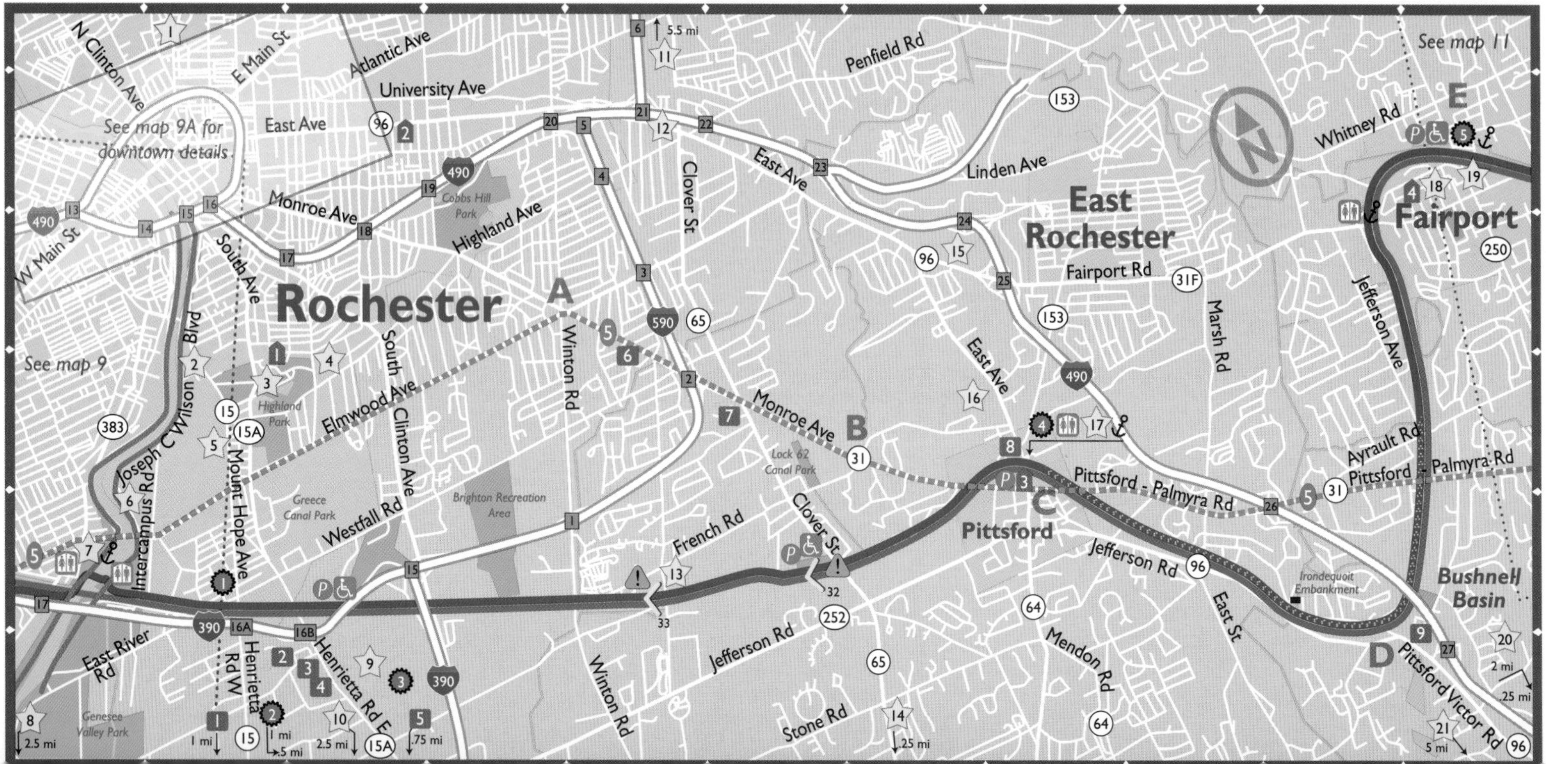

See map 11

E
Fairport
250

18
19

Whitney Rd
Jefferson Ave

Ayrault Rd
Palmyra Rd

Pittsford
31
5

Bushnell
Basin
20   2 mi   25 mi

9   Pittsford Victor Rd
27
96
21   5 mi

D

Marsh Rd

26

Irondequoit
Embankment

East St

Pittsford – Palmyra Rd
96

East
Rochester

Fairport Rd
31F

153

490
17
4

8

C
Pittsford

Jefferson Rd

Mendon Rd
64

64

Linden Ave
153

East Ave

East Ave
25
16

24
15
96
23

Penfield Ave

Clover St
22
21
12

Clover St
65
590
3
5   6

490
19

Cobbs Hill
Park

A
Rochester

Highland Ave

University Ave
96   2

Monroe Ave
7
2

Lock &
Canal Park

Monroe Ave
31   **B**

31

Clover St
32
(252)

French Rd
13

Jefferson Rd
65

Stone Rd
14   25 mi

Winton Rd
33

Winton Rd
1

N

Brighton
Recreation
Area

Atlantic Ave
East Ave

Monroe Ave
18

South Clinton Ave

Elmwood Ave
Westfall Rd

Greece
Canal Park

390

Henrietta Rd E
9
10   2.5 mi   (15A)
5   .75 mi

E Main St
N Clinton Ave

See map 9A for
downtown details.

South Ave
15   (15A)
5

Highland
Park
4
3

Mount Hope Ave

16B
2   3   4
16A
Henrietta
Rd W
(15)
2   1 mi   .5 mi

390
1   1 mi

W Main St
490
13

See map 9

Joseph C Wilson Blvd
2

Intercampus Rd
6

383

15
15A
14
15

17

Genesee
Valley Park

East River Rd
East Ave

8   2.5 mi

THINGS TO SEE & DO

1	Rochester Public Market	280 North Union Street	(585) 428-6907
2	Ellwanger Garden	625 Mount Hope Avenue	(585) 546-7029
3	Lamberton Conservatory	Highland Park	(585) 256-4950
4	Colgate Rochester Divinity School		(585) 271-1320
5	Mount Hope Cemetery	1133 Mount Hope Ave	(585) 342-1516
6	University of Rochester	Intercampus Drive	(585) 275-2121
7	Canoe Livery at Genesee Valley Park	Genesee River Shore	(585) 428-6755
8	Rochester Institute of Technology	1 Lomb Memorial Drive	(585) 475-2411
9	Monroe County Community College	1000 East Henrietta Rd	(585) 292-2000
10	Monroe County Fairgrounds	2695 East Henrietta Rd	(585) 334-4000
11	Seabreeze Amusement Park	4600 Culver Road	(585) 323-1900
12	Stone Tolan House Museum	2370 East Avenue	(585) 546-7029
13	Jewish Community Center for the Arts	1200 Edgewood Avenue	(585) 461-2000
14	Tinker Homestead Farm & Museum	1585 Calkins Road	(585) 359-7042
15	St John Fisher College	3690 East Avenue	(585) 385-8000
16	Nazareth College	4245 East Avenue	(585) 389-2525
17	Schoen Place Shops		(585) 334-4000
18	Fairport Historical Museum	18 Perrin Street	(585) 223-3989
19	Colonial Belle Cruises	400 Packetts Landing	(585) 223-9470
20	Casa Larga Vineyards	2287 Turk Hill Road	(585) 223-4210
21	Ganondagan Historic Site	1488 State Route 444	(585) 924-5848

TRAIL & TRAVEL NOTES

Schoen Place — Pittsford's Schoen Place is a bustling group of specialty shops and restaurants right on the trail. Several canal-related buildings, including an old coal tower converted into a restaurant, are in evidence. Pittsford's Main Street, with interesting architecture and shopping, is just a short walk from Schoen Place. Cyclists must walk their bikes through Schoen Place.

The Great Embankment — To carry the canal above the floor of the Irondequoit Creek Valley, a 70-foot-high, mile-long fill area was constructed. When you see tree tops practically level with the trail a few miles east of Pittsford, you'll know you're traversing this canal skyway, commonly known as the "Great Embankment."

Cycling Tips — ⚠ Take care walking your bicycle down the very steep steps adjacent to Locks 33 and 32.

Pittsford's Schoen Place waterfront

SERVICE AREAS

A	🅿	$	ℹ	Rx	✕	🚻	
B	🅿	$	ℹ	Rx	✕	🚻	🛒	🔧
C	🅿	$	ℹ			🚻		🛒
D	🅿	$	ℹ			🚻		
E	🅿	$	ℹ		✕	🚻	🚻	

45

MAP 11   FAIRPORT – PALMYRA

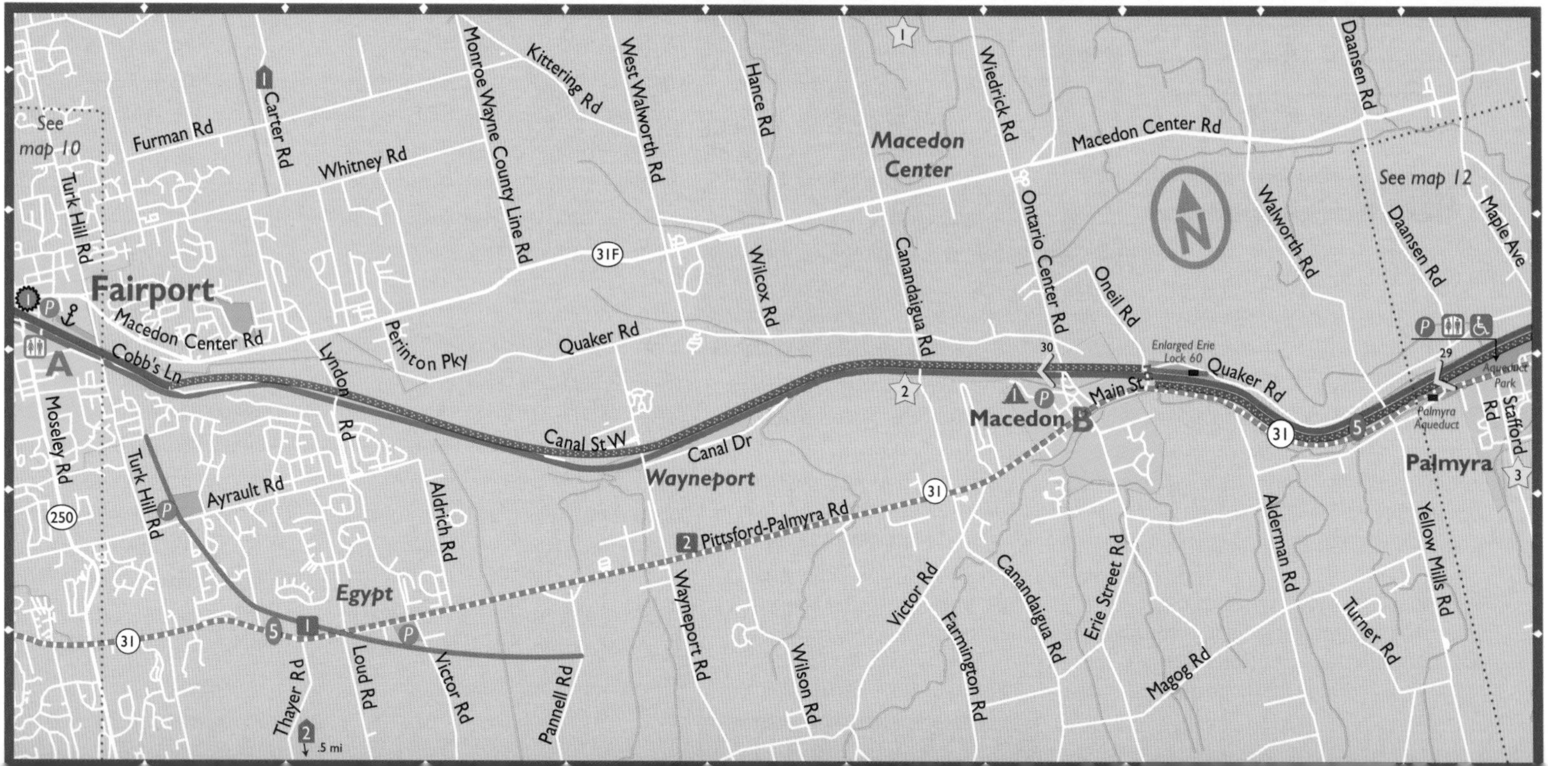

Maple Ave

Stafford Rd 3

See map 12

Daansen Rd

P 29

Palmyra Aqueduct

Palmyra

Yellow Mills Rd

Daansen Rd

Walworth Rd

Turner Rd

5

Alderman Rd

31

Quaker Rd

Macedon Center Rd

Oneil Rd

Enlarged Erie Lock 60

Main St

Macedon B

Erie Street Rd

Maog Rd

Wiedrick Rd

Ontario Center Rd

30

P

Macedon

Canandaigua Rd

Macedon Center

Canandaigua Rd

2

31

Farmington Rd

Victor Rd

Hance Rd

Wilcox Rd

Canal Dr

Wayneport

Pittsford-Palmyra Rd

Wilson Rd

West Walworth Rd

Kittering Rd

Quaker Rd

Canal St. W

Wayneport Rd

31F

Monroe Wayne County Line Rd

Pannell Rd

Whitney Rd

Perinton Pky

Aldrich Rd

Victor Rd

Egypt

P

Furman Rd

Lyndon Rd

Ayrault Rd

Loud Rd

5

Thayer Rd

2 .5 mi

Carter Rd

Fairport

Macedon Center Rd

Cobb's Ln

Turk Hill Rd

250

31

See map 10

Turk Hill Rd

P

A

Moseley Rd

THINGS TO SEE & DO

1	Amazing Maize Maze at Long Acre Farms	1342 Eddy Road	(315) 986-4202
2	Mid-Lakes Navigation Canal Boat Rentals	Erie Canal at Canandaigua Road	(315) 685-8500
3	Joseph Smith Home & Sacred Grove	863 Stafford Road	(315) 597-1671

A lift bridge in action

TRAIL & TRAVEL NOTES

Lift Bridges — The original canal bridges were just a few feet above the water, thus the common warning "low bridge, everybody down." As commerce increased and towns grew, new bridges, such as lift bridges, were constructed. The easternmost of the 16 remaining lift bridges, designed to "lift up" out of the way of canal boats, is found in Fairport. The Fairport lift bridge is unusual in that it slopes because the opposite canal banks are at different elevations.

Renewal Along the Canal — Fairport is among the towns again looking to the canal for economic prosperity. Since 1981, Fairport has invested more than $1 million in canalside improvements and the village's thriving waterfront demonstrates that this effort is paying off.

Iroquois Confederacy — About seven miles south of Fairport is Ganondagan State Historic Site, the capital of the Seneca Nation and the westernmost edge of the Iroquois Confederacy. The Senecas were the most numerous and powerful of the Five Nations of the Iroquois Confederacy.

Bikes and boats in Fairport's canal harbor

SERVICE AREAS

A	$	Rx			
B	$	Rx			

47

MAP 12   PALMYRA – NEWARK

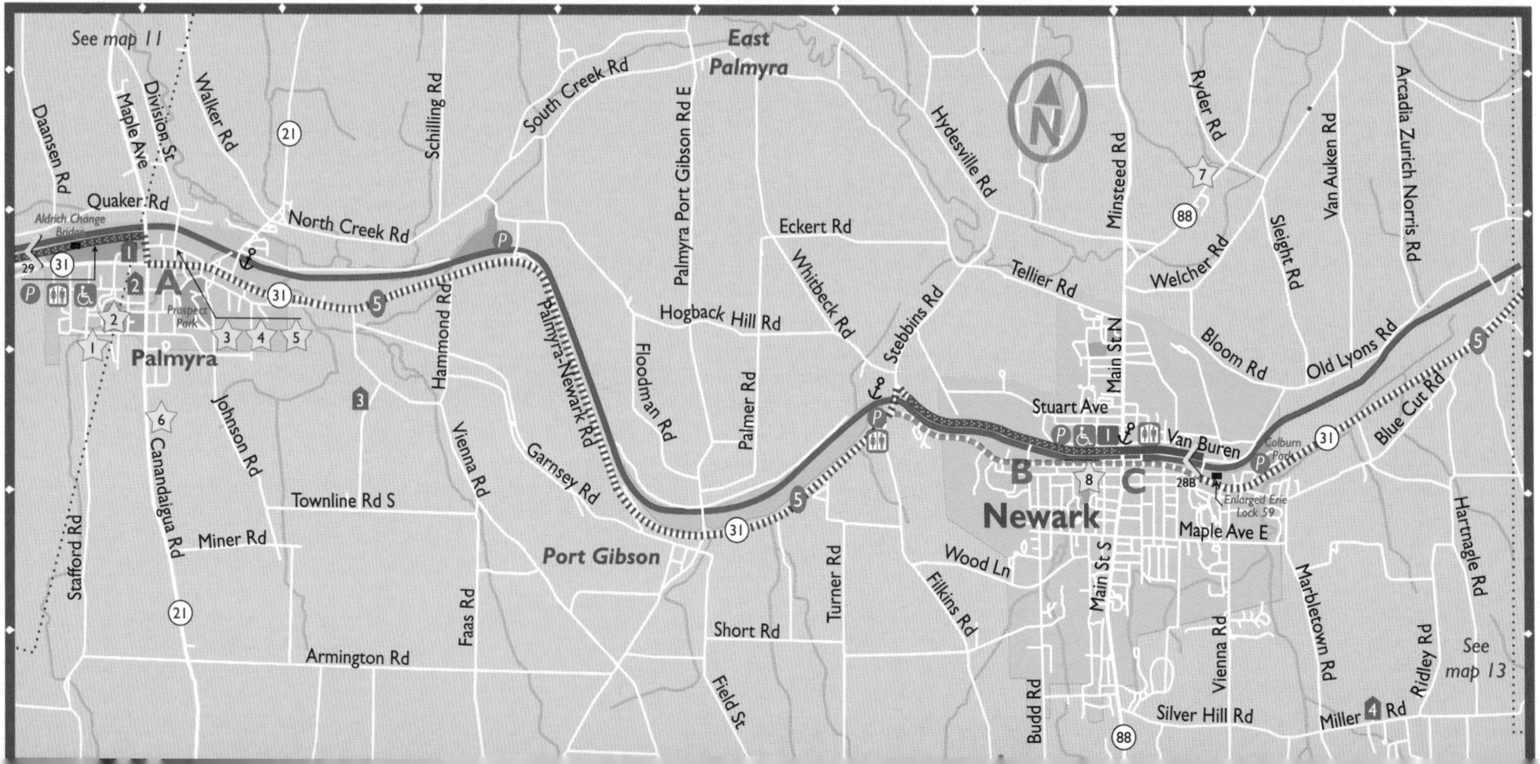

Arcadia Zurich Norris Rd

Hartnagle Rd

See map 13

Ridley Rd

Miller Rd

Van Auken Rd

Sleight Rd

Old Lyons Rd

Blue Cut Rd

Marbletown Rd

Ryder Rd

Welcher Rd

Bloom Rd

Van Buren

Maple Ave E

Vienna Rd

Silver Hill Rd

Minsteed Rd

Tellier Rd

Stuart Ave

Main St N

Newark

B
C

Main St S

Budd Rd

Hydesville Rd

Wood Ln

Filkins Rd

Stebbins Rd

East
Palmyra

Eckert Rd

Whitbeck Rd

Palmer Rd

Turner Rd

Hogback Hill Rd

Short Rd

Field St

Palmyra Port Gibson Rd E

Floodman Rd

Port Gibson

South Creek Rd

Palmyra-Newark Rd

Garnsey Rd

Schilling Rd

Hammond Rd

Vienna Rd

Faas Rd

North Creek Rd

Townline Rd S

Armington Rd

Walker Rd

Johnson Rd

Miner Rd

Canandaigua Rd

Palmyra

Division St

Maple Ave

Quaker Rd

Daansen Rd

Aldrich Change

See map 11

Stafford Rd

THINGS TO SEE & DO

1. Joseph Smith Home & Sacred Grove — 863 Stafford Road — (315) 597-1671
2. Wayne County Fairgrounds — West Foster Street — (315) 597-5372
3. Alling Coverlet Museum — 122 William Street — (315) 597-6737
4. Historic Palmyra Museum — 132 Market Street — (315) 597-6737
5. Grandin Building — 217 East Main Street — (315) 597-5982
6. Hill Cumorah Site & Visitor Center — 603 State Route 21 — (315) 597-5851
7. Newark Farmers' Market — 1581 Route 88 North — (315) 331-8415
8. Hoffman Clock Museum — 121 High Street — (315) 331-4370

Pageant scene at Hill Cumorah

TRAIL & TRAVEL NOTES

Religious Revivalism — During the 1820s and '30s, religious revivalism swept through western New York with such intensity that the area was called the "Burned Over District." Evangelical sects and new religious groups such as the Latter Day Saints and Seventh Day Adventists began in canal communities and spread along the waterway.

Birthplace of Mormon Church — Palmyra is the birthplace of Mormon Church founder Joseph Smith. Visitors can tour the Joseph Smith house and other Mormon-related museums and sites, including Hill Cumorah, the site of a popular annual Mormon pageant.

Aldrich Change Bridge — Change bridges allowed horses and mules to cross the canal when the towpath switched from one side to the other without being unhitched and re-hitched. The Aldrich change bridge, designed by premier American bridge designer Squire Whipple, is one of only two such bridges to survive today. Originally located in Rochester, the restored bridge now resides in Palmyra-Macedon Aqueduct Park.

SERVICE AREAS

A | $ 🏧 Rx 🍴 🛏 🚤 🎫 🏕
B | $ 🏧 Rx 🍴 🛏 🎫
C | $ 🏧 Rx 🍴 🎫 🚤 🔧

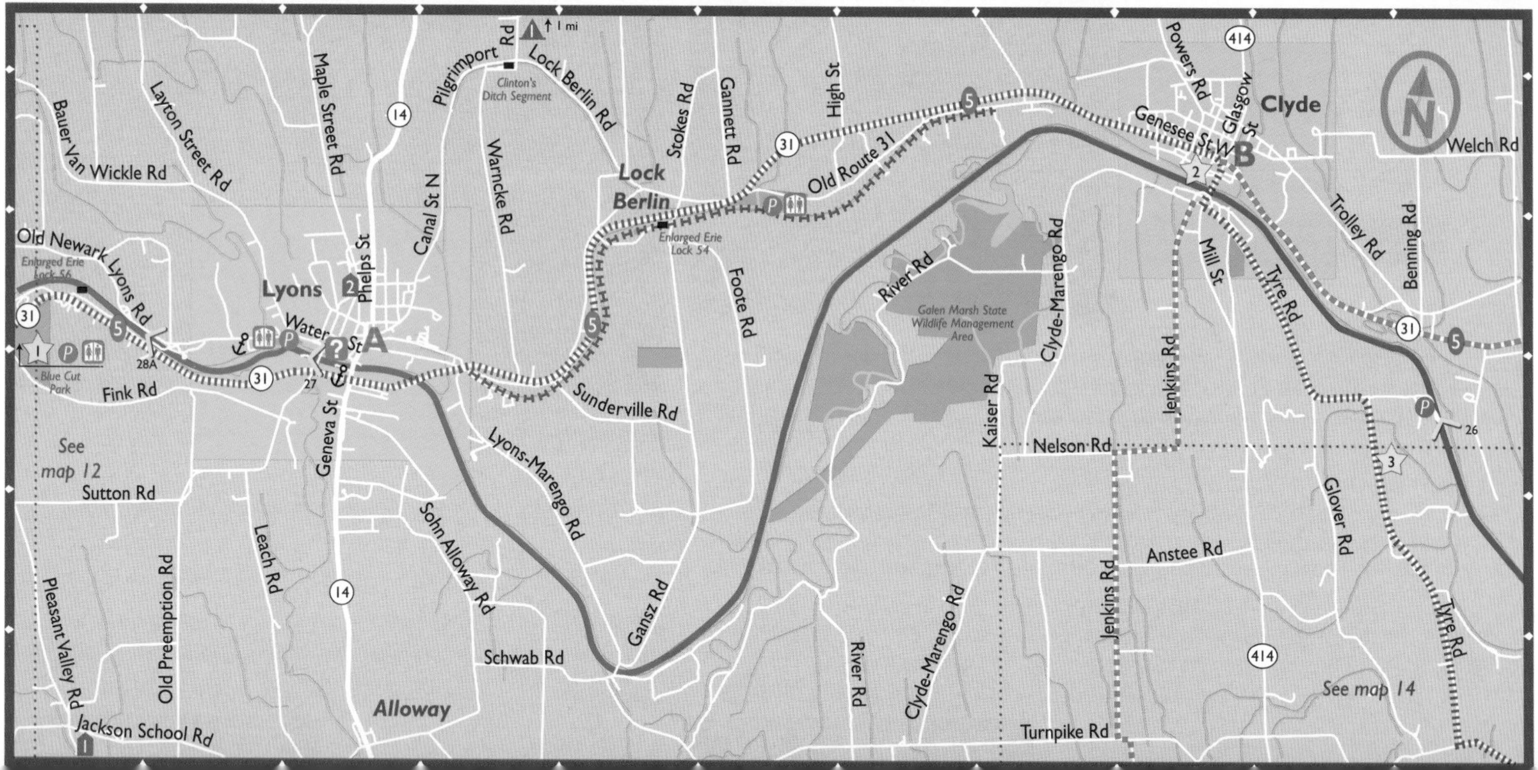

MAP 13 LYONS – CLYDE

N

Welch Rd

Clyde

414

Powers Rd

Genesee St

Glasgow St

Trolley Rd

Benning Rd

31

5

26

P

3

Tyre Rd

Tyre Rd

Glover Rd

See map 14

414

Mill St

Jenkins Rd

Nelson Rd

Anstee Rd

Clyde-Marengo Rd

Jenkins Rd

Turnpike Rd

Kaiser Rd

River Rd

Clyde-Marengo Rd

Gohen Marsh State Wildlife Management Area

River Rd

High St

Old Route 31

31

P

Gannett Rd

Foote Rd

Stokes Rd

Berlin

Lock

Enlarged Erie Lock 54

Sunderville Rd

Ganzs Rd

Lock Berlin Rd

Warncke Rd

Canal St N

Lyons-Marengo Rd

Schwab Rd

Pilgrimport Rd

Clinton's Ditch Segment

1 mi

14

Maple Street Rd

Phelps St

Water St

Geneva St

Sohn Alloway Rd

Alloway

14

Lyons

P

27

31

Leach Rd

Layton Street Rd

Old Newark Lyons Rd

Fink Rd

28A

See map 12

Sutton Rd

Old Preemption Rd

Jackson School Rd

Pleasant Valley Rd

Bauer Van Wickle Rd

Enlarged Erie Lock 56

31

P

Blue Cut Park

THINGS TO SEE & DO

1	Blue Cut Nature Center	581 Route 88 North	(315) 331-8415
2	Galen Historical Society	Sodus Street	
3	Grape Hill Lilac Gardens	1232 Tyre Road	

Lock Berlin Park

TRAIL & TRAVEL NOTES

Erie Canal Engineering — Many challenges had to be overcome when constructing the Erie Canal through Western New York: cutting through the Niagara Escarpment, crossing the Genesee River, getting over the Irondequoit Creek Valley, and traversing the Great Montezuma Swamp. Canal engineers met all these challenges, figuring out and refining their techniques as the canal progressed. These engineers went on to construct other canals, railroads, and public water supplies throughout the expanding nation.

Peppermint Production — Peppermint grew well in the low, mucky soil around Lyons. Thousands of acres of the crop were planted and processed into high-quality peppermint oil, in high demand throughout Europe.

Cycling Tips — The main Erie Canalway Trail route continues east on Bike Route 5 but the alternate route south to Waterloo and Seneca Falls shown on the map in gray boxes is highly recommended.

VISITOR INFORMATION

Wayne County Office of Tourism
Lyons • (315) 946-5469
9 Pearl Street • www.tourism.co.wayne.ny.us

Village square in Clyde

SERVICE AREAS

A	$ ⑪ Rx	📖	⚒ ↙
B	$ ⑪ Rx	🍴 🛍	↘ ↙

MAP 14 MONTEZUMA MARSH

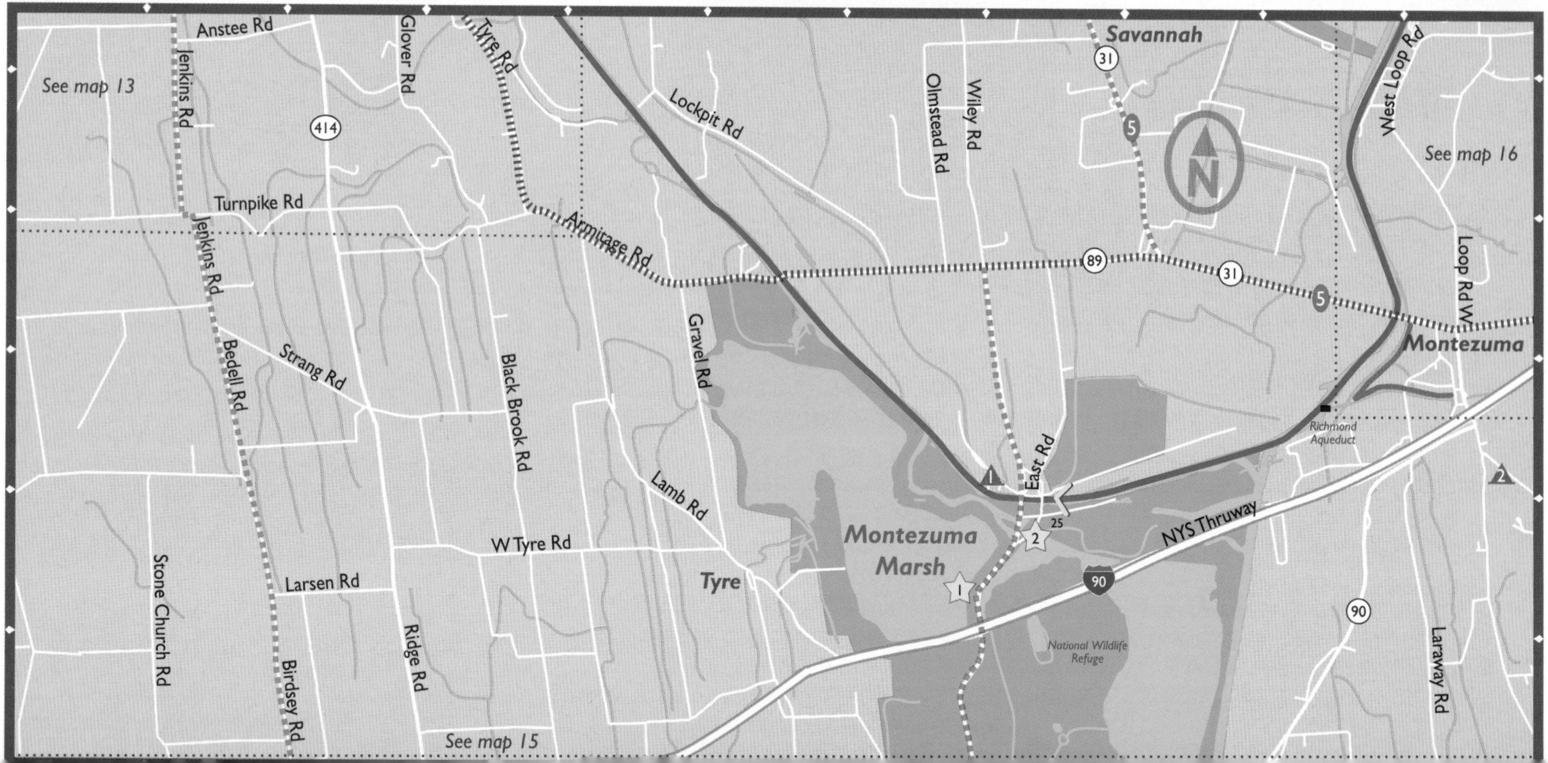

See map 16

Loop Rd W.

Montezuma

Laraway Rd

West Loop Rd

Richmond Aqueduct

NYS Thruway

5

31

90

Savannah

31

5

69

90

National Wildlife Refuge

East Rd

25

2

Wiley Rd

Olmstead Rd

Montezuma Marsh

1

Lockpit Rd

Gravel Rd

Lamb Rd

Tyre

Armitage Rd

Tyre Rd

Black Brook Rd

W Tyre Rd

See map 15

Glover Rd

Ridge Rd

414

Strang Rd

Larsen Rd

Birdsey Rd

Anstee Rd

Turnpike Rd

Jenkins Rd

Bedell Rd

Jenkins Rd

Stone Church Rd

See map 13

THINGS TO SEE & DO

1 Montezuma Marsh
   National Wildlife Refuge   Tschache Pool Viewing Tower – Route 89   **(315) 568-5987**

2 Montezuma Marsh
   National Wildlife Refuge   Mays Point Pool Viewing Area – Route 89   **(315) 568-5987**

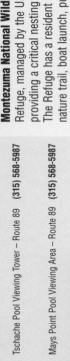

An Amish farmstead sits amidst a small but flourishing local Amish community

TRAIL & TRAVEL NOTES

Montezuma National Wildlife Refuge — The 7,000-acre Montezuma National Wildlife Refuge, managed by the U.S. Fish and Wildlife Service, is a link in the Atlantic flyway, providing a critical nesting and resting spot for migratory waterfowl and other birds. The Refuge has a resident bald eagle population. Facilities include a visitor center, nature trail, boat launch, public fishing site, and observation towers.

Getting the canal through the Great Swamp — Thousands of Irish immigrants were employed to dig the canal through Montezuma, then called the "Great Cayuga Swamp." So many contracted malaria and other mosquito-borne diseases, however, that digging was finally postponed until winter.

Cycling Tips — At the present time, bicycling is not permitted in Montezuma National Wildlife Refuge.

Great Blue Heron at Montezuma Marsh

A sea of green in Montezuma Marsh

53

Laraway Rd

Baldwin Rd

Genesee St Rd W

Cayuga Rd

Chappell Rd

Cayuga

Willard St

20 5

90

N

5

CS 1

12

Montezuma Marsh

National Wildlife Refuge

Auburn Rd

Demonts Rd

5

89

Lower Lake Rd

Cayuga Lake State Park

3 ?

89

6

Hyatt Rd

Tyre Rd E

Lay Rd

11

318

George Rd

5

20

5

Auburn Rd

Gravel Rd

7

8

9

4

3

2

CS 2 & 3

Bayard St E

10

4

Garden St

Seneca Falls

318

318

Black Brook Rd

5

6

5

4

3

Fall St

2 ?

20

C

90

414

Mound Rd

North Rd

2

3

B

2

River Rd

318

Burgess Rd

Birdsey Rd

Gassner Rd

Powderly Rd

Mills Rd

96

Waterloo

1

A

CS 4

Main St W

20

See map 14

1 2

2

THINGS TO SEE & DO

1	Memorial Day Museum	35 East Main Street	(315) 539-0533
2	Montezuma Winery	2981 Auburn Road	(315) 568-8190
3	Women's Rights National Historic Park	136 Fall Street	(315) 568-2991
4	Seneca Falls - Heritage Area Visitors' Center	115 Fall Street	(315) 568-2703
5	Seneca Museum of Waterways & Industry	89 Fall Street	(315) 568-1510
6	National Women's Hall of Fame	76 Fall Street	(315) 568-8060
7	Seneca Falls Historical Society	55 Cayuga Street	(315) 568-8412
8	Erie Canal Cruise Lines	Seneca Falls Harbor	(800) 962-1771
9	Liberty Boat Tours	Seneca Falls Harbor	(877) 472-6668
10	Elizabeth Cady Stanton Home	32 Washington Street	(315) 568-2991
11	Montezuma Marsh National Wildlife Refuge Spring Pools	East Tyre Road	(315) 568-5987
12	Montezuma Marsh National Wildlife Refuge Visitor Center	3395 State Route 5/20	(315) 568-5987

Boating the Cayuga-Seneca Canal to the Finger Lakes

TRAIL & TRAVEL NOTES

Social reform on the canal — The Erie Canal was a channel for ideas as well as goods and people. Two of the most significant social reform movements of the 19th century – abolition and women's rights – began and spread along the canal.

Women's rights — Seneca Falls is known as the birthplace of the suffragist movement, as the first women's rights convention was held there in 1848. The National Women's Hall of Fame honors and celebrates the achievements of distinguished American women, while the Women's Rights National Historical Park chronicles the development of the movement that finally led to women getting the vote in 1920.

Cayuga-Seneca Canal — The Cayuga-Seneca Canal extends from Geneva to Montezuma, skirting two of New York's Finger Lakes, Cayuga Lake and Seneca Lake. Eventually, a 19-mile multi-use trail will follow the Canal from Seneca Lake at Geneva through Waterloo and Seneca Falls to the Montezuma National Wildlife Refuge, where it will join the Erie Canalway Trail.

VISITOR INFORMATION

Seneca County Chamber of Commerce
Seneca Falls • (315) 568-2906
2020 State Route 5/20 • www.senecachamber.org

Seneca Falls Heritage Area Center
Seneca Falls • (315) 568-2703
115 Fall Street • www.nps.gov/wori/ucp.htm

Cayuga Lake State Park
Seneca Falls • (315) 568-5163
2678 Lower Lake Road

SERVICE AREAS

A	$	10	Rx	🍴	🏪	⛽	🔧
B	$	10	Rx	🍴	🏪	⛽	🔧
C	$	10	Rx	🍴	🏪	⛽	🔧

MAP 16 PORT BYRON – WEEDSPORT

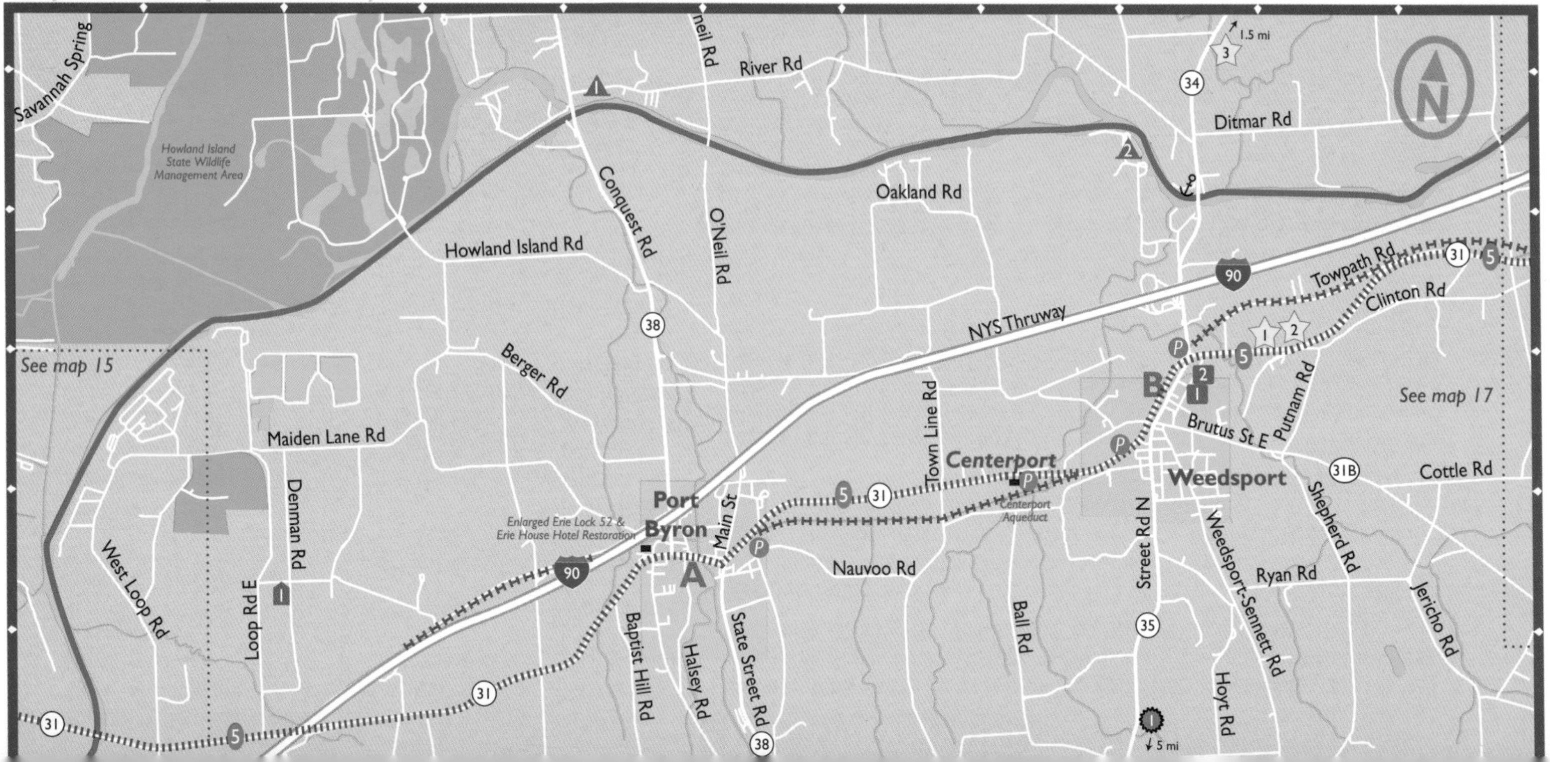

N

Ditmar Rd

34

1.5 mi

3

90

River Rd

neil Rd

Oakland Rd

NYS Thruway

O'Neil Rd

Conquest Rd

38

Howland Island Rd

Berger Rd

Howland Island State Wildlife Management Area

Savannah Spring

See map 15

Maiden Lane Rd

Denman Rd

1

Loop Rd E

West Loop Rd

5

31

90

Enlarged Erie Lock 52 & Erie House Hotel Restoration

Baptist Hill Rd

Halsey Rd

State Street Rd 38

Main St

A

P

Port Byron

Nauvoo Rd

Ball Rd

Town Line Rd

Centerport

Centerport Aqueduct

5

31

Street Rd N

35

↓ 5 mi

Hoyt Rd

Weedsport-Sennett Rd

Ryan Rd

Weedsport

Shepherd Rd

31B

Cottle Rd

Jericho Rd

See map 17

Brutus St E

Putnam Rd

1 2

5

90

Towpath Rd

Clinton Rd

31 / 5

P

B

2

1

P

THINGS TO SEE & DO

1	Cayuga County Fairgrounds & Speedway	1 Speedway Drive - Route 31	(315) 834-6606
2	DIRT Motorsports Hall of Fame & Classic Car Museum	1 Speedway Drive - Route 31	(315) 834-6667
3	Giancarelli Brothers Winery	10252 Shortcut Road	(315) 626-2830

Rolling upstate farmland

TRAIL & TRAVEL NOTES

A legacy of prosperity — Communities such as Port Byron bustled with activity during the heyday of the canal. As boats crowded the waterfronts of communities up and down the canal, wagons of goods and carriages of travelers made their way along the roads to and from the canal.

Finger Lakes — New York's Finger Lakes region is south of here. During the most recent Ice Age, a one-mile-thick sheet of ice gouged a series of long, thin lakes shaped like fingers. The area is dotted with wineries, as the deep lakes' moderating effect on local temperatures creates ideal conditions for grape growing. Although many types of grapes are grown, the region's Rieslings are particularly notable.

Cycling Tips — About eight miles north of Weedsport, at Cato, a 15-mile rail-trail extends to Lake Ontario. For more information on this trail and other multi-use trails in New York, visit Trail Finder Maps, Parks & Trails New York's on-line guide to muli-use trails, at www..ptny.org.

Artistic depiction of bustling village during heyday of Erie Canal

SERVICE AREAS

A	$	🏨	📖	🍴
B	$	🏨		🍴

MAP 17 JORDAN – CAMILLUS

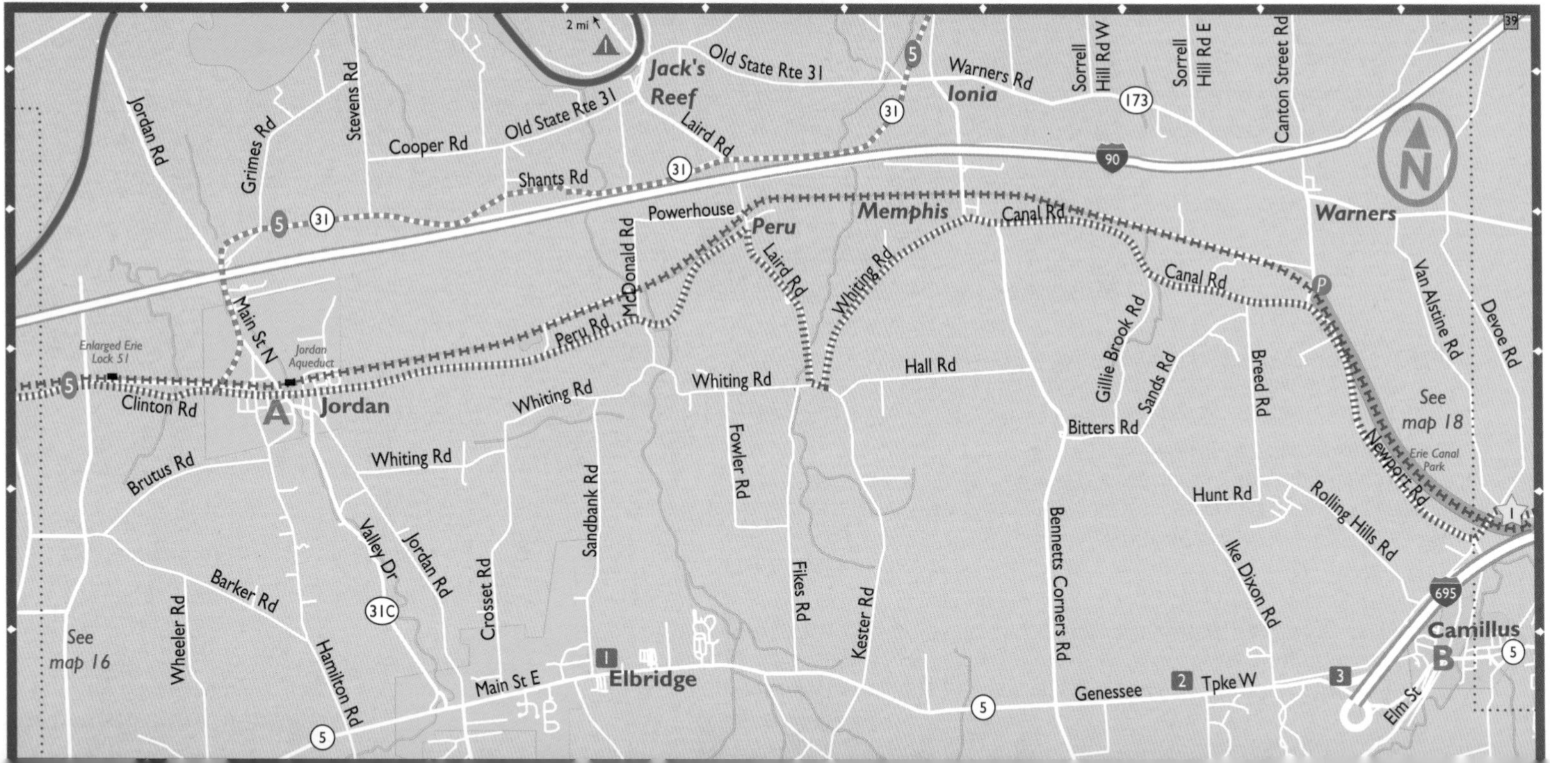

Devoe Rd

Van Alstine Rd

See
map 18

Warners

Erie Canal
Park

Newport Rd

Camillus

5

695

Elm St

B

Canton Street Rd

Sorrell Hill Rd E

Sorrell Hill Rd W

173

90

Warners Rd

Ionia

Breed Rd

Canal Rd

Sands Rd

Gillie Brook Rd

Bitters Rd

Rolling Hills Rd

Hunt Rd

Ike Dixon Rd

2 Tpke W

Genessee

Bennetts Corners Rd

3

5

5

Old State Rte 31

31

Jack's
Reef

Laird Rd

31

Memphis

Canal Rd

Whiting Rd

Peru

Laird Rd

Powerhouse

McDonald Rd

Hall Rd

Whiting Rd

Fowler Rd

Kester Rd

Fikes Rd

Elbridge

1

Main St E

2 mi

Old State Rte 31

31

Shants Rd

Peru Rd

Whiting Rd

Sandbank Rd

Crosset Rd

Cooper Rd

Stevens Rd

Whiting Rd

Jordan Rd

Valley Dr

31C

Hamilton Rd

5

Grimes Rd

5

Jordan
Aqueduct

A

Jordan

Main St N

Clinton Rd

Brutus Rd

Barker Rd

Wheeler Rd

See
map 16

Jordan Rd

Enlarged Erie
Lock 51

5

THINGS TO SEE & DO

1 Sims Store Museum   Devoe Road   (315) 488-3409

TRAIL & TRAVEL NOTES

Sims Store — Camillus, the halfway point on the original Erie Canal, is home to the 300-acre Camillus Erie Canal Park. Built and maintained largely through the efforts of volunteers, the park includes seven miles of restored towpath and navigable canal, a reproduction lock tender's shanty, and the Sims Store Museum, a replica of an 1860s canalside store.

Nine Mile Creek Aqueduct — The Nine-Mile Creek Aqueduct was one of 32 aqueducts constructed, as part of the first enlargement of the Erie Canal, to carry the canal and towpath over rivers, ravines, and roads. Typically, the stone arches of an aqueduct supported the towpath, while the canal itself was carried in a wooden trough resting on stone piers. The original masonry of Nine Mile Creek Aqueduct is still in place and plans are underway to restore the structure. When completed, it will be the only navigable aqueduct of the original 32.

SERVICE AREAS

A $ 🚻 ♿

B $ 🏳 🚲

Nine-Mile Creek Aqueduct

Historic image of aqueduct with intact timbers

Natural surface canal trail near Weedsport

59

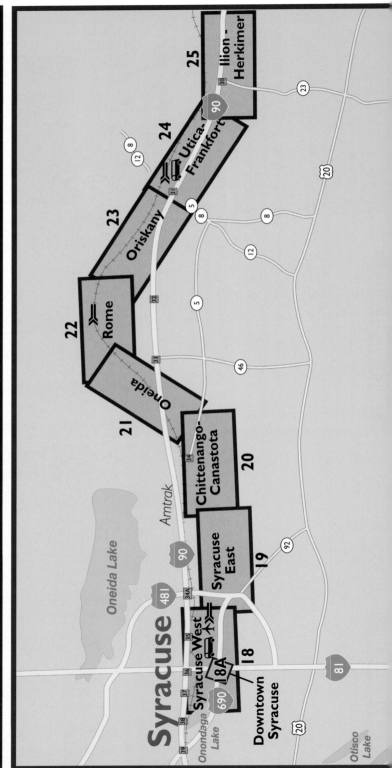

COMMUNITIES ALONG ROUTE

Onondaga County	Jordan, Camillus, Syracuse, Fayetteville
Madison County	Chittenango, Canastota, Oneida
Oneida County	Oneida, Rome, Oriskany, Whitesboro, Utica
Herkimer County	Frankfort, Ilion, Mohawk, Herkimer

VISITOR INFORMATION

Onondaga County	www.visitsyracuse.org	(800) 234-4797
Madison County	www.madisontourism.com	(800) 684-7320
Oneida County	www.oneidacountycvb.com	(800) 426-3132
Herkimer County	www.herkimercountychamber.com	(877) 984-4636

SAFETY & SECURITY

Universal Emergency Number: 911

State Police

Troop D	Onondaga, Madison, Oneida, & Herkimer Counties	(315) 366-6000

County Sheriff

Onondaga	(315) 435-3044
Madison	(315) 366-2318
Oneida	(315) 736-0141
Herkimer	(315) 867-1167

TRANSPORTATION

Amtrak Rail Stations

Syracuse (SYR)	131 P&C Parkway	(315) 477-1152
Rome (Unstaffed) (ROM)	6599 Martin Street	
Utica (UCA)	321 Main Street	(315) 797-8962

Bus Stations

Regional Transportation Center – Syracuse	131 P&C Parkway	(315) 477-1152
Birnie Bus & 4-County Line Runs – Rome	7944 Upper West Thomas St	(315) 336-3950
Trailways Ticket Office – Utica	321 Main Street	(315) 797-2550

Urban & Regional Transit

Central New York Transportation Authority	Port Byron to Fayetteville	(315) 442-3400
	www.centro.org	
Utica Transit Authority	Whitesboro to Utica	(315) 797-1121
	www.borg.com/~myozouta/	

Commercial Airports

Syracuse Hancock International (SYR)	www.syrairport.org	(315) 454-4330

Regional / Local Airports & Airfields

Michael Airfield Airport (1G6)	Cicero
Luther Airport (1D5)	Chittenango
Griffiss Airpark Airport (RME)	Rome
Becks Grove Airport (K16)	Rome
Oneida County Airport (UCA)	Utica
Frankfort Highland Airport (6B4)	Frankfort

MAP 18 SYRACUSE WEST

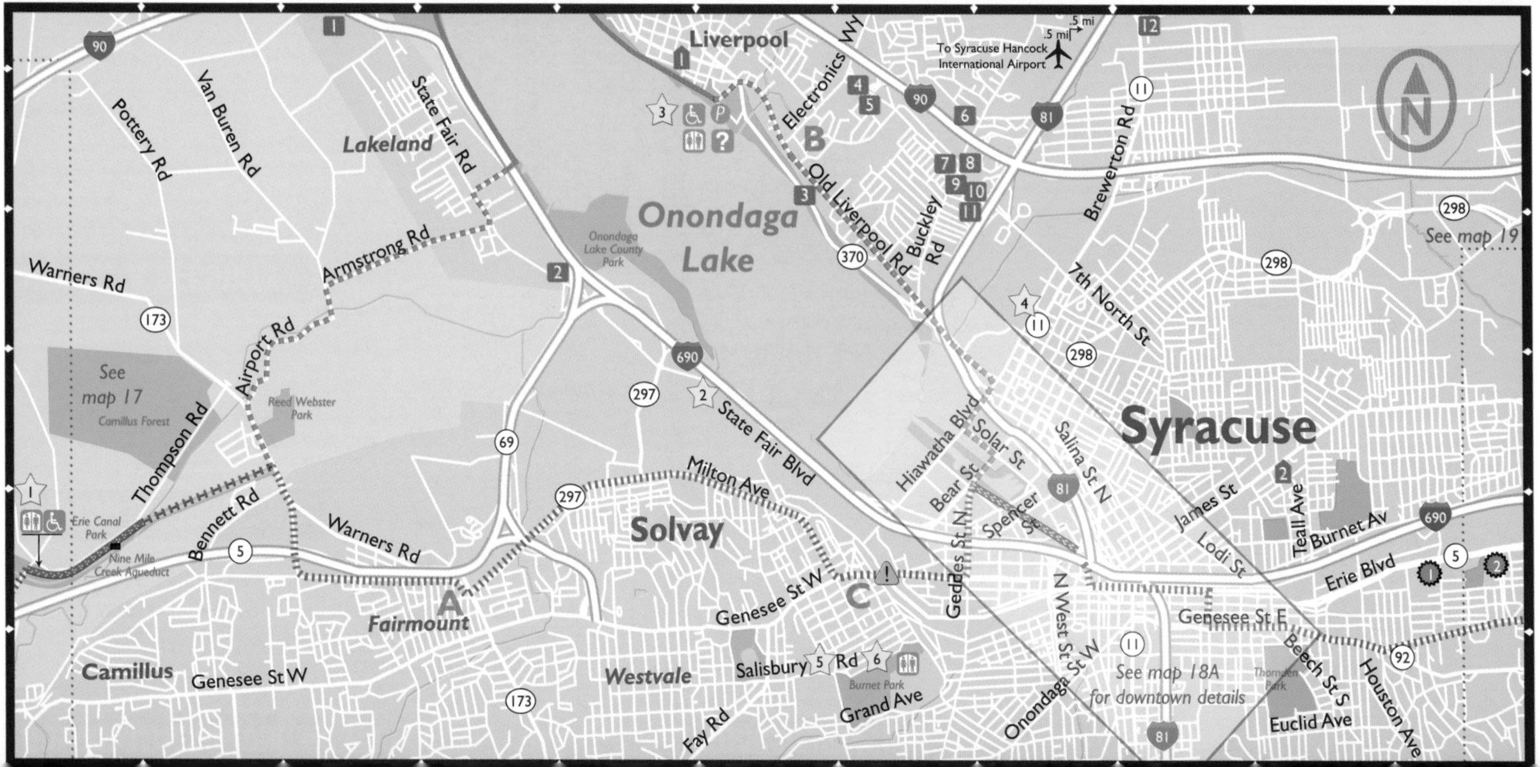

See map 19

See map 18A for downtown details

Syracuse

Liverpool

Solvay

Westvale

Fairmount

Camillus

Lakeland

Onondaga Lake

Onondaga Lake County Park

To Syracuse Hancock International Airport

5 mi

See map 17

Camillus Forest

Reed Webster Park

Nine Mile Creek Aqueduct

Erie Canal Park

298
690
5
92
81
11
12
6
90
370
297
2
69
173
5
90

Houston Ave
Burnet Ave
Teall Ave
Erie Blvd
Beech St S
Euclid Ave
Genesee St E
Thornden Park
Burnet Park
Grand Ave
James St
Lodi St
Salina St N
7th North St
Brewerton Rd
Spencer
Solar St
Bear St
Geddes St N
Hiawatha Blvd
N West St
Onondaga St W
Salisbury Rd
Fay Rd
Genesee St W
Genesee St W
Milton Ave
State Fair Blvd
State Fair Rd
Armstrong Rd
Airport Rd
Bennett Rd
Thompson Rd
Warners Rd
Van Buren Rd
Pottery Rd
Warners Rd
Old Liverpool Rd
Buckley Rd
Electronics Pkwy

N

THINGS TO SEE & DO

1	Sims Store Museum	Devoe Road	(315) 488-3409
2	Expo Center - State Fairgrounds	580 State Fair Boulevard	(315) 487-7711
3	Salt Museum	Onondaga Lake Park	(315) 453-6767
4	Skychiefs Baseball at P&C Stadium	1 Tex Simone Dr	(315) 474-7833
5	James Pass Arboretum	Avery Avenue & Salisbury Road	(315) 473-4330
6	Rosamond Gifford Zoo	1 Conservation Place - Burnet Park	(315) 435-8511

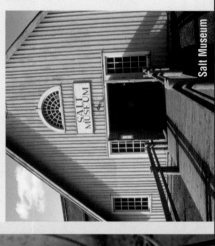

Livestock in competition at the state fair

TRAIL & TRAVEL NOTES

Syracuse and salt — For many years during the mid 19th century, Syracuse supplied the bulk of the salt used in America. First, salt was processed by boiling brine from swamps around Onondaga Creek; later, large shallow vats were constructed to take advantage of solar evaporation. With the opening of the Erie Canal and then the Oswego Canal (which provided direct access to Lake Ontario), Syracuse industries rapidly diversified from salt to steel, cars, guns, gears, typewriters, beer, and even bicycles.

New York State Fair — Each year, nearly one million people visit the New York State Fair, which has been entertaining New Yorkers and other visitors since 1841.

Cycling Tips — ⚠ Traffic is heavy and room for bicycles is marginal on the route into downtown Syracuse.

Salt Museum

VISITOR INFORMATION

Joseph Griffin Visitor Center
Liverpool • (315) 453-6712
Onondaga Lake County Park
http://onondagacountyparks.com

SERVICE AREAS

A	$	⊕	Rx		🛏	🔧
B	$	⊕	Rx		🛏	
C	$	⊕			🧺	

Onondaga Lake

Regional Transportation Center (Bus & Amtrak)

1

370

Hiawatha Blvd

Wolf St

81

Lemoyne St

Carbon St
Spring St
First North St

Bean St

N Salina St
Park St
Lodi St

Turtle St

Court St

298

Danforth St

Kirkpatrick St

Steuben St

Spencer St
Pulaski St
Van Rensselaer St
Solar St
Bear St
Onondaga Creek
Creekwalk

W Kirkpatrick St

2

P

21

22

Spencer St

Lilac St

Pond St

9 9

690

10

W Belden St

N Geddes St

Park Ave
Wilkinson St

W Genesee St

Mary St

John St

S Alvord St
Park St

Solar St

N Clinton St

N State St

N Salina St

N Townsend St

Erie Blvd W

5

N West St

3

Franklin Sq.

!

11 12

20

N Ash St

Butternut St

4

Lodi St

Catherine St

Mardellus St
Otisco St
Tully St
Wyoming
West St
Seymour St

W Onondaga

6

7

Erie Blvd E

W Washington St

8

P

9

I

10

11

E Jefferson St

13 12

13

5

E Laurel St

Hickory St

E Willow St N

McBride St

James St

2

290

E Onandaga St

P

14

15

16

P

P

II

?
S Clinton St
S Salina St

Montgomery St

S State St

Butternut St

S Townsend St

S McBride St

3

Madison St

Harrison St

E Adams St

Irving Ave

Hawley Ave

Burner Ave

Green St

Gertrude St

E Water St
E Washington St

E Fayette St

690

5

E Raynor Ave

18

81

S Crouse Ave

Marshall St
Waverly Ave

University Ave

University Pl

17

Walnut Ave

Comstock Ave

Ostrom Ave

E Genesee St

4

5

Thornden Park

18 Syracuse University

THINGS TO SEE & DO

#	Name	Address	Phone
1	Central NY Farmers Market	2100 Park Street	(315) 422-8647
2	Syracuse Inner Harbor	Solar Street	(315) 448-2244
3	Franklin Square Historic District		
4	International Mask and Puppet Museum	518 Prospect Avenue	(315) 476-0466
5	Ner-A-Car Antique NY Motorcycles Collection	478 N Salina Street	(315) 472-7931
6	Museum of Auto History	321 N Clinton Street	(315) 478-2277
7	Clinton Square		
8	Armory Square Entertainment District		
9	Museum of Science and Technology / Bristol Imax	500 S Franklin Street	(315) 425-9068
10	Ontrack City Express Train	269 W Jefferson Street	(315) 424-1212
11	Landmark Theater	362 S Salina Street	(315) 475-7980
12	Erie Canal Museum & Heritage Area	318 Erie Boulevard E	(315) 471-0593
13	Syracuse City Hall	Montgomery Street & Water St	(315) 448-8005
14	Onondaga Historical Museum	321 Montgomery Street	(315) 428-1864
15	OnCenter Performance & Entertainment Complex	411 Montgomery Street	(315) 435-2121
16	Everson Museum of Art	401 Harrison Street	(315) 474-6064
17	Syracuse University & Lowe Art Gallery	University Place	(315) 443-4098
18	Carrier Dome	900 Irving Avenue	(315) 443-4634

TRAIL & TRAVEL NOTES

Inner Harbor — Located in a former barge canal terminal and maintenance facility, the Inner Harbor is the centerpiece in the overall redevelopment plan for the Syracuse Lakefront. Still a work in progress, the Inner Harbor, with an inlet from the Erie Canal at Lake Onondaga, offers boating facilities, a restaurant, a promenade, and an amphitheatre that hosts special events throughout the summer.

Armory and Franklin Squares — By the early 20th century, Syracuse outranked New York City in the production of manufactured goods. Neighborhoods such as Armory Square and Franklin Square grew into diverse manufacturing quarters. Today, historic Armory Square offers quaint shops and restaurants, while Franklin Square is a charming mixed-use neighborhood with old-fashioned street lamps, brick sidewalks, and ornamental ironwork.

Erie Canal Museum — Housed in the 1850 Weighlock Building, designed to weigh canal boats for assessment of tolls, the Erie Canal Museum has hands-on exhibits that provide visitors with insight into the canal's development and its impact on everyday people's lives. A featured exhibit is a full-scale replica of a 100-foot canal boat.

Cycling Tips — Cyclists might want to avoid the southern end of the Onondaga Creekwalk in favor of adjacent streets due to the presence of several sets of stairs.

Clinton Square

VISITOR INFORMATION

Erie Canal Museum & Heritage Area
318 Erie Boulevard E • (315) 471-0593
www.eriecanalmuseum.org

Syracuse Convention & Visitors Bureau
572 S Salina Street • (315) 470-1910
www.syracusecvb.org

MAP 19 **SYRACUSE EAST**

66

.5 mi

James St

Kirkville Rd

East
Syracuse

690

Erie Blvd

Thompson Rd

5

Salt Springs Rd

Radcliffe Rd

Genesee Sr E

92

See
map 18

Randall Rd

Nottingham Rd

Fremont Rd

Manlius Center Rd

Richmond Rd

290

Minoa

Baird St

Burdick St N

Manlius Center Rd

Fremont Rd

Towpath Rd

Orrick Rd

Kinne Rd

A 2

DeWitt

481

Richdorf
Park

Woodchuck Hill Rd

Cedar Bay Rd

Ryder
Park

Cedar Bay
Park

Limestone Creek
Aqueduct

Old Erie
Canal S.P.

Genesee St E

3

92

Highbridge Rd

Manlius Rd

Old Erie Canal S.P.

Manlius Rd N

257

Fayetteville

B

5

4

D

Salt Springs Rd

Fayetteville Manlius Rd

257

Green Lake Rd

290

2

Green Lakes
State Park

Genesee St E

Salt Springs Rd

Eagle Village Rd N

Kinderhook Rd

Poolsbrook Rd N

Poolsbrook Rd

Kirkville
Rd

Kirkville

Kirkville Rd

290

Old Erie Canal S.P.

?

Genesee Tpke

Gulf Rd

5

Palmer Rd

Seneca Tpke E

Salt Springs Rd

Townsend Rd

See
map 20

N

THINGS TO SEE & DO

1	Lemoyne College & Wilson Art Gallery	1419 Salt Springs Road	(315) 445-4100
2	Green Lakes State Park	7900 Green Lakes Road	(315) 637-6111

TRAIL & TRAVEL NOTES

Old Erie Canal State Historic Park — Old Erie Canal State Historic Park, managed by the NYS Office of Parks, Recreation and Historic Preservation, is a 36-mile linear park running from DeWitt to Rome. Water still flows through this old segment of the Erie Canal, making for tranquil canoeing and kayaking. The National Park Service designated the park a National Recreational Trail.

Green Lakes State Park — Green Lakes State Park is named for its two glacial lakes of an astounding aquamarine color. Both Green Lake and Round Lake (a National Natural Landmark) are deep-water meromictic lakes, meaning that there is no fall and spring mixing of surface and bottom waters. The lakes and surrounding uplands provide a variety of recreational opportunities, including an 18-hole golf course.

Cycling Tips — ⚠ Take care crossing busy, six-lane Erie Boulevard (Route 5). In Old Erie Canal State Park be prepared to share the trail as horses (and snowmobiles in winter) are permitted.

Intact canal segments in Old Erie Canal State Historic Park make for great paddling

Riding the "Enlarged Erie" towpath through Old Erie Canal State Historic Park

VISITOR INFORMATION

Green Lakes State Park
Fayetteville • (315) 637-6111
7900 Green Lakes Road

SERVICE AREAS

A	$	⑪	Rx	⛟	🍴	🚻	⛽
B	$	⑪	Rx	⛟	🛒	🚻	⛽
C	$	⑪	⛽				

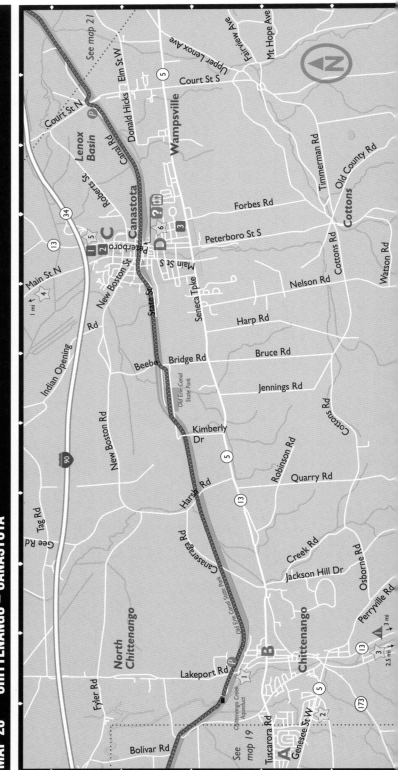

See map 21

Court St N

Court St S

Upper Lenox Ave

Fairview Ave

Mt Hope Ave

Donald Hicks

Elm St W

Lenox Basin

Canal Rd

Roberts St S

Canastota

Wampsville

Forbes Rd

Timmerman Rd

Old County Rd

Cottons

Peterboro

New Boston St

Main St N

Indian Opening

Peterboro St S

Cottons Rd

Nelson Rd

State St

Main St S

Seneca Tpke

Harp Rd

Bruce Rd

Watson Rd

New Boston Rd

Beebe

Bridge Rd

Old Erie Canal State Park

Jennings Rd

Kimberly Dr

Cottons Rd

Robinson Rd

Quarry Rd

Harsh Rd

Gee Rd

Tag Rd

Canaseraga Rd

Old Erie Canal State Park

Creek Rd

Jackson Hill Dr

Osborne Rd

Fyler Rd

North Chittenango

Chittenango

Perryville Rd

Lakeport Rd

Chittenango Creek Aqueduct

See map 19

Bolivar Rd

Tuscarora Rd

Genesee St W

3 mi

2.5 mi

1 mi

THINGS TO SEE & DO

1	Chittenango Landing Canal Boat Museum	7010 Lakeport Road	(315) 687-3801
2	L. Frank Baum Museum	227 W Genesse Street	(315) 687-3423
3	Chittenango Falls State Park	2300 Rathbun Road	(315) 655-9620
4	Great Swamp Conservancy Nature Center	8375 N Main Street	(315) 697-2950
5	International Boxing Hall of Fame	360 N Peterboro Street	(315) 697-7095
6	Canastota Canal Town Museum	122 N Canal Street	(315) 697-3451

TRAIL & TRAVEL NOTES

Chittenango Landing Canal Boat Museum — During the 19th and 20th centuries, Chittenango Landing had a facility to build and repair 100-foot-long canal boats. The Canal Boat Museum, another great example of a canal restoration project spearheaded by volunteers, tells of the construction of these boats and the workings of the restored dry docks, the only ones surviving from the era of the original "Clinton's Ditch" canal.

Follow the yellow brick road — *Wizard of Oz* author L. Frank Baum was born in Chittenango. The yellow brick sidewalks in the village, a small museum, and an annual Oz Festival commemorate this native son.

International Boxing Hall of Fame — Sports fans will enjoy Canastota's Boxing Hall of Fame, featuring gloves, robes, videos, ticket stubs, and other boxing memorabilia. Carmen Basilio, world welterweight and middleweight champion in the 1940s, comes from Canastota.

VISITOR INFORMATION

Canastota Chamber of Commerce
Canastota • (315) 697-3677
222 South Peterboro Street • www.canastota.org

SERVICE AREAS

A	$	🏨	📖
B	🏨	Rx 🍴 🍺 🍷 🏕	📧 🔧
C	$	🏨	
D	$	🏨 Rx 🍴 🍷	📧

Old dry docks at Chittenango Landing Canal Boat Museum

Shops in downtown Canastota

MAP 21 **ONEIDA**

70

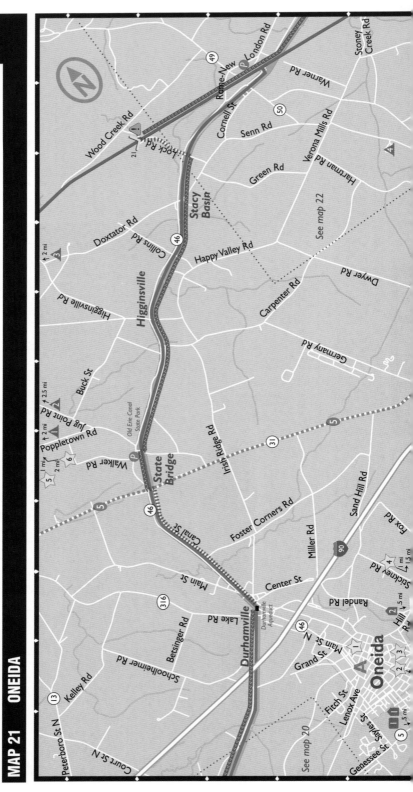

THINGS TO SEE & DO

1	Greater Oneida Kallet Civic Center	159 Main Street	(315) 363-8525
2	Shako:wi Cultural Center & Oneida Indian Nation	5 Territory Road	(315) 363-1424
3	Madison County Historical Society	435 Main Street	(315) 363-4136
4	Turning Stone Casino	5218 Patrick Road	(315) 365-7469
5	Sylvan Beach Amusement Park	112 Bridge Street	(315) 762-5212
6	Verona Beach State Park	Route 13	(315) 762-4463

Culverts such as this allowed small streams to pass under the canal.

TRAIL & TRAVEL NOTES

Oneida Community — Founded in 1848 by John Humphrey Noyes and his followers, the "Oneida Perfectionists," this utopian community eschewed individual ownership, both of material goods and spouses. The prosperity and cosmopolitan nature of the Erie Canal corridor created a climate of social innovation and experimentation in which places such as the Oneida Community could flourish. Guided tours are available of the sprawling National Historic Landmark Community Mansion House, built to meet the needs of several hundred people living together as one family. Oneida Ltd. today continues the tradition of fine silverware begun by the Oneida Community.

Rome Sand Plains — This environmentally and biologically unique area west of Rome features a combination of high parabolic sand dunes and low peat bogs that support a specialized community of rare plants and animals.

Cycling Tips — ⚠ The trail route crosses over the top of the downstream gate of Lock 21. Walk your bike, watch for gaps, and enjoy the unique view of a lock chamber.

The trail route crosses the gate at Lock 21.

SERVICE AREAS

⛺ $ ⊕ Rx 🍴 👕 🛏 🛒 🔧

71

MAP 22 ROME

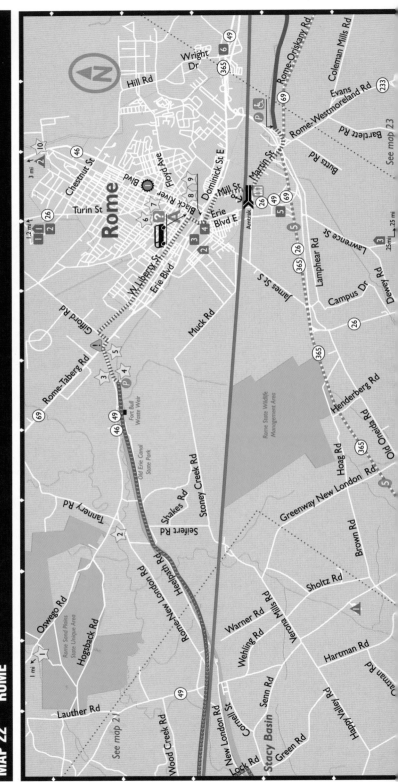

THINGS TO SEE & DO

1 Beck's Grove Dinner Theater	4286 Oswego Road	(315) 336-7038
2 Fort Rickey Childrens Discovery Zoo	5135 Rome New London Rd	(315) 336-1930
3 Peterpaul Recreation Park	Rome New London Road	(315) 339-2666
4 Erie Canal Village	5789 Rome New London Rd	(315) 339-7755
5 Rome Sports Hall of Fame & Museum	5790 Rome New London Rd	(315) 339-9038
6 Rome Art and Community Center	308 W Bloomfield Street	(315) 336-1040
7 Jervis Library	613 N Washington Street	(315) 336-4570
8 Rome Historical Society Museum	200 Church Street	(315) 336-5870
9 Fort Stanwix National Monument	112 E Park Street	(315) 336-2090
10 Delta Lake State Park	8797 State Route 46	(315) 337-4670

Erie Canal Village

TRAIL & TRAVEL NOTES

Start of canal construction — For political, strategic, and geologic reasons, construction of the Erie Canal did not begin at either end, but in the middle. Starting in Rome offered several advantages: the flat topography made it possible to build many miles of canal without locks; progress was quicker because one crew could go west and one crew east; and the eager towns on either end helped ensure the project's completion.

Erie Canal Village — This re-creation of a mid-19th century canal community features boat rides in a mule-drawn packet boat on a section of the historic canal.

Fort Stanwix — Constructed to protect the western headwaters of the Mohawk River during the French and Indian War, the original Fort Stanwix also played a key role in the Revolutionary War. Fort Stanwix National Monument, a reconstruction of the fort managed by the National Park Service, provides a glimpse of life in an 18th century military outpost.

Cycling Tips — ⚠ Take care when crossing Route 69 (Erie Boulevard) because of high traffic volume and speed.

Fort Stanwix National Monument

VISITOR INFORMATION

Rome Chamber of Commerce
Rome • (315) 337-1700
139 W Dominick Street • www.romechamber.com

SERVICE AREAS

A $ ⑩ Rx 🏠 🍴 🛏 ⛽ 🛒 ✉ 🔧

MAP 23 ORISKANY

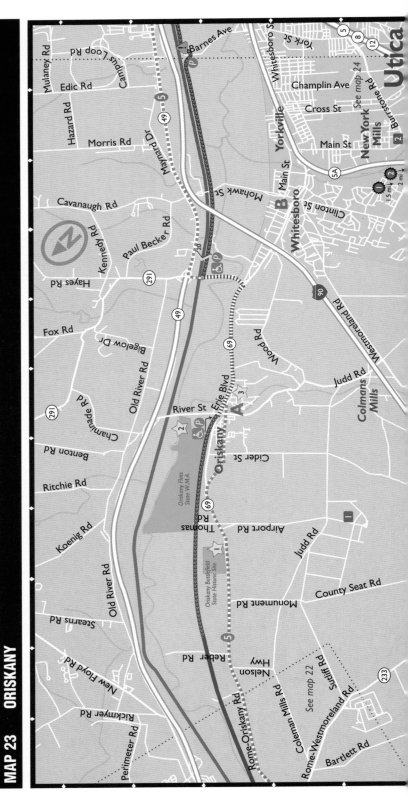

Mulaney Rd
Edic Rd
Campus Loop Rd
Barnes Ave
York St
Whitesboro St
5
8
12
Utica

Hazard Rd
Morris Rd
Maynard Dr
5
49
Champlin Ave
Cross St
Main St
See map 24
Burrstone Rd
2

Cavanaugh Rd
Kennedy Rd
Paul Becker Rd
Mohawk St
Yorkville
Main St
Whitesboro
New York Mills
5A
1.5 mi
2 mi

Hayes Rd
Fox Rd
Bigelow Dr
Old River Rd
291
49
20
P
Whitesboro
Clinton St
90
Westmoreland Rd

Champeade Rd
291
Benton Rd
Ritchie Rd
River St
Erie Blvd
69
Wood Rd
A
3
Judd Rd
Colmans Mills

Koenig Rd
Old River Rd
Oriskany Flats State W.M.A.
2
P
Oriskany
Cider St
69

Stearns Rd
Thomas Rd
Oriskany Battlefield State Historic Site
1
Airport Rd
Judd Rd
1

New Floyd Rd
Rickmyer Rd
Perimeter Rd
Old River Rd
Reber Rd
Nelson Hwy
5
69
Monument Rd
County Seat Rd

Rome-Oriskany Rd
Coleman Mills Rd
Rome-Westmoreland Rd
See map 22
Sutliff Rd
Bartlett Rd
233

THINGS TO SEE & DO

1 Oriskany Battlefield State Historic Site	7801 State Route 69	(315) 768-7224
2 Oriskany Flats Wildlife Management Area	River Street	(315) 793-2554
3 Oriskany Village Museum	420 Utica Street	(315) 736-7529

Oriskany Battlefield monument

Wetland views abound along the Canalway Trail

TRAIL & TRAVEL NOTES

Mohawk Valley — Stretching from Central New York to the Hudson River, this broad, scenic valley is the only water-level passage through the Appalachians. This has made it a focal point for the movement of people and goods for thousands of years, starting with Native Americans, through fur traders and colonial settlers, to modern Americans.

Oriskany Battlefield State Historic Site — The Battle of Oriskany, one of the bloodiest of the Revolutionary War, was pivotal to the success of the American effort. Had the Americans not stood their ground here, British troops might have reached the Hudson River Valley and joined up with other British forces from the west and east to overpower the Americans at Saratoga and cut off New England from the rest of the colonies. A memorial marks the battle site, which is a National Historic Landmark.

Cycling Tips — ⚠ Be careful crossing the railroad tracks along this stretch of trail east of the boat launch.

Bike touring is fun for the whole family

SERVICE AREAS

A	🅿 🍴 ▸
B	$ 🅿 Rx 🚻 📷 🛏 ▸

75

MAP 24   UTICA – FRANKFORT

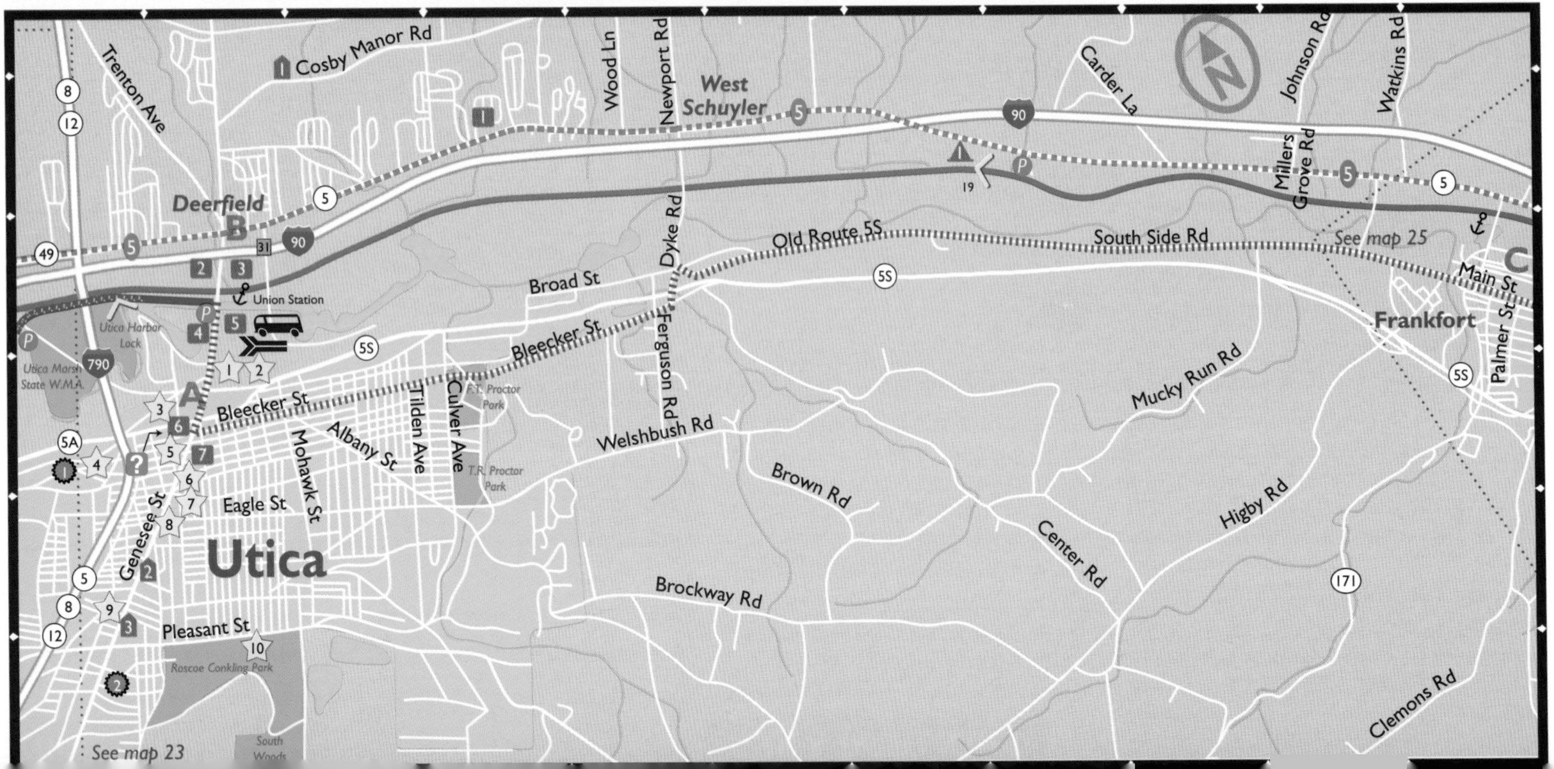

Frankfort

Main St

Palmer St

Watkins Rd

Johnson Rd

Millers Grove Rd

Carder La

South Side Rd

Mucky Run Rd

Higby Rd

Clemons Rd

Center Rd

Brown Rd

Brockway Rd

West Schuyler

Newport Rd

Wood Ln

Cosby Manor Rd

Deerfield

Trenton Ave

Old Route 5S

Dyke Rd

Ferguson Rd

Welshbush Rd

Broad St

Bleecker St

Bleecker St

Culver Ave

Tilden Ave

Albany St

Mohawk St

Eagle St

Pleasant St

Genesee St

Utica

Union Station

Union Harbor Lock

See map 25

See map 23

T.R. Proctor Park

F.T. Proctor Park

Utica Marsh State WMA

South Woods

Roscoe Conkling Park

THINGS TO SEE & DO

1	Children's Museum	311 Main Street	(315) 724-6129
2	Adirondack Scenic Railroad	Union Station	(315) 724-0700
3	Utica Memorial Auditorium	400 Oriskany Street	(315) 738-0164
4	F.X. Matt Brewery Tour Center	830 Varick Street	(315) 732-0022
5	National Distance Running Hall Of Fame	114 Genesee Street	(315) 724-4525
6	Stanley Performing Arts Center	259 Genesee Street	(315) 724-4000
7	Mohawk Valley Ballet	261 Genesee Street	(315) 738-7646
8	Munson-Williams-Proctor Arts Institute	310 Genesee Street	(315) 797-0000
9	Oneida County Historical Society	1608 Genesee Street	(315) 735-3642
10	Utica Zoo	99 Steele Hill Road	(315) 738-0472

Munson-Williams-Proctor Institute

TRAIL & TRAVEL NOTES

Two-Canal Town — The section of Erie Canal between Rome and Utica was the first to be open for operation in 1819. Utica's location on the Erie and later the Chenango Canal, which extended to Binghamton and the Susquehanna River Valley, led to its development as an important commercial and industrial center, known for its textiles.

Art and Architecture — The Munson-Williams-Proctor Art Institute houses an acclaimed collection of 18th to 20th century fine arts in a 1960s International Style building designed by Philip Johnson.

Adirondacks by Rail — Vintage excursion trains leave Utica from Amtrak's restored 1914 Union Station to travel north through the scenic Adirondacks to Thendara near Old Forge. The only New York Central steam locomotive on public display is located at Union Station.

F.X. Matt Brewery - a great place for a break

See map 24

See map 26

90

5

5

167

55

Jacksonburg

90

5

18

Oregon Rd

Quinn Rd

Miller Rd

Shoemaker Hill Rd

Griffin Rd

Shoemaker Rd

Gun Club Rd

Eatonville Rd

Bush Rd

Smalls

Pine Grove Rd

Lock 18 State Wildlife Management Area

5   4

East Herkimer

Folts Rd

Canada Creek

28

Herkimer

Steuben Hill Rd

Mc Kennan Rd

Main St

State St

W German St

3

3   2

3

2

2   2

55

3

Putts Hill Rd

Columbia St

Mohawk

168

28

N

Main St E

5

Russell Park

1

Warren Rd

Bell Hill Rd

Main St W

Frankfort

Acme Rd

Main St W

Palmer St

4th Ave

171

55

Reese Rd

Barringer Rd

Mc Gowan Rd

5th Ave

2nd St

Otsego St

Ilion

Avery Rd

51

3

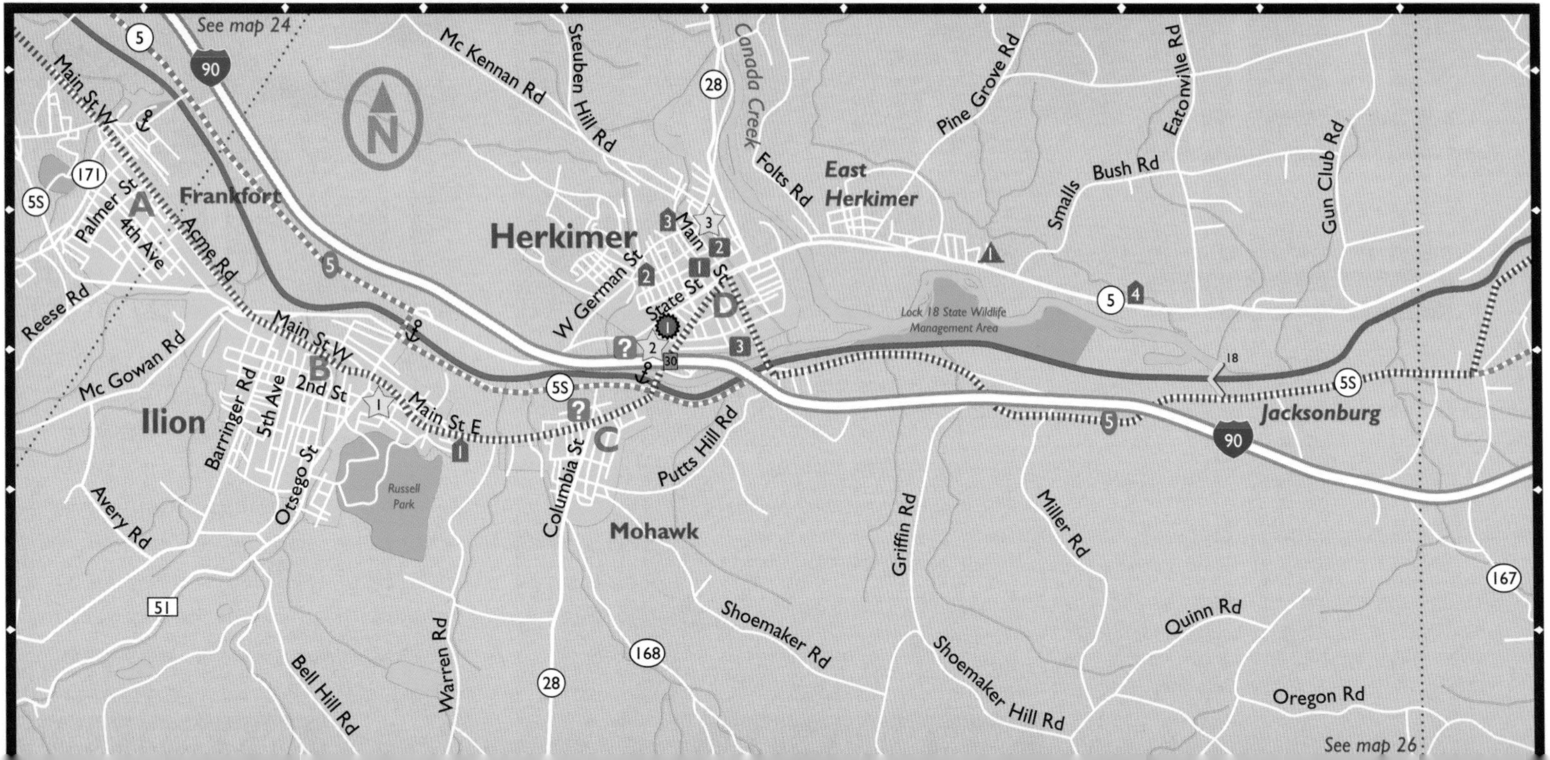

THINGS TO SEE & DO

1	Remington Firearms Plant & Museum	Hoefler Avenue & Catherine Street	(315) 895-3200
2	Gems Along the Mohawk & Canal Cruises	800 Mohawk Street	(315) 717-0077
3	Herkimer County Historical Society	400 N Main Street	(315) 866-6413

Historic gun display at Remington Firearms Museum

Historic image of Remington Arms factory

TRAIL & TRAVEL NOTES

Industrial Giant — When Eliphalet Remington relocated his rifle factory to the Canal in 1828, he launched Ilion as a major industrial center that would be known for firearms, typewriters, and many other manufactured goods. Tours of the 175-year old Remington Firearms Plant and exhibits at the Remington Firearms Museum illustrate the city's extensive manufacturing history.

Dairying and Diamonds — Mohawk Valley soils are well suited for pastureland and dairying. Cheese making was an important industry and area canal towns, most notably Little Falls, became major centers for the shipment of cheese. Seven miles north of Herkimer, you can dig in open mines for sparkling quartz crystals known as "Herkimer Diamonds."

Changes to River and Canal — Today, from Rome to Waterford, the Erie Canal is located primarily within the bed of the Mohawk River. Until 1918, the canal ran in a separate cut parallel to the river. At that time, newer construction techniques allowed the river's powerful waters to be dammed and controlled and its bottom "channelized" to accommodate larger diesel barges. These improvements extended the working era of the canal until 1959, when the opening of the St. Lawrence Seaway created a more direct and economical route to the Great Lakes.

VISITOR INFORMATION

Herkimer County Chamber of Commerce
Mohawk • (315) 866-7820
28 West Main Street
www.herkimercountychamber.com

Oneida County Convention & Visitors Bureau
Herkimer • (315) 724-7221
800 Mohawk Street • www.leatherstockingny.org

SERVICE AREAS

A	$	Rx			
B	$	Rx			
C	$				
D	$	Rx			

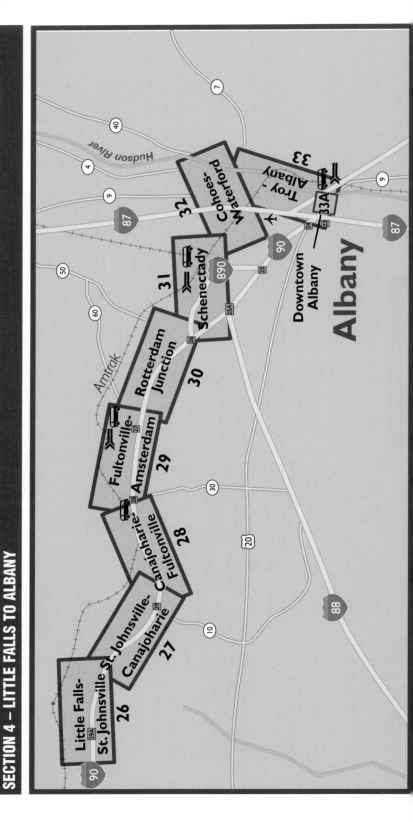

COMMUNITIES ALONG ROUTE

Herkimer County	Little Falls
Montgomery County	St. Johnsville, Fort Plain, Nelliston, Palatine Bridge, Canajoharie, Fonda, Fultonville, Amsterdam
Schenectady County	Scotia, Schenectady
Saratoga County	Waterford
Albany County	Cohoes, Green Island, Watervliet, Menands, Albany
Rensselaer	Troy, Rensselaer

VISITOR INFORMATION

Herkimer County	www.herkimercountychamber.com	(877) 984-4636
Montgomery County	www.montgomerycountyny.com	(800) 743-7337
Schenectady County	www.schenectadychamber.org	(800) 962-8007
Saratoga County	www.saratoga.org	(518) 584-3255
Albany County	www.albany.org	(800) 258-3582
Rensselaer County	www.rensco.com	(518) 270-8667

SAFETY & SECURITY

Universal Emergency Number: 911

State Police

Troop D	Herkimer County	(315) 366-6000
Troop G	Montgomery, Schenectady, Albany, Saratoga, & Rensselaer Counties	(518) 783-3211

County Sheriff

Herkimer	(315) 867-1167
Montgomery	(518) 853-3435
Schenectady	(518) 388-4300
Saratoga	(518) 885-2250
Albany	(518) 487-5400
Rensselaer	(518) 270-5448

TRANSPORTATION

Amtrak Rail Stations

Utica (UCA)	321 Main Street	(315) 797-8962
Amsterdam (AMS)	466 West Main Street	(518) 842-4451
Schenectady (SDY)	332 Erie Boulevard	(518) 346-8651
Albany/Rensselaer (ALB)	525 East Street	(518) 462-5740

Bus Stations

Union Station – Utica	321 Main Street	(315) 797-2550
Dairy Bar – Fonda	22 Bridge Street	(518) 853-4433
Travel Center – Schenectady	1120 Riverfront Center	(518) 842-8760
Amsterdam Travel	22 State Street	(518) 346-3415
Albany Bus Terminal	34 Hamilton Avenue	(518) 436-9651

Urban & Regional Transit

Capital District Transportation Authority	Schenectady to Rensselaer	(518) 482-8822
	www.cdta.org	

Commercial Airports

Albany International (ALB)	www.albanyairport.com	(518) 242-2200

Regional / Local Airports & Airfields

Dolgeville Airport (1F6)	Dolgeville
Sharon Airport (K31)	Sharon Springs
Duanesburg Airport (4B1)	Duanesburg
Mohawk Valley Airport (K13)	Scotia
Schenectady County Airport (SCH)	Scotia
Round Lake Airport (W57)	Round Lake
Saratoga County Airport (5B2)	Saratoga Springs
Burrello-Mechanicville Airport (K27)	Mechanicville
Rensselaer County Airport (5B7)	Troy
South Albany Airport (4B0)	Bethlehem

MAP 26   LITTLE FALLS – ST. JOHNSVILLE

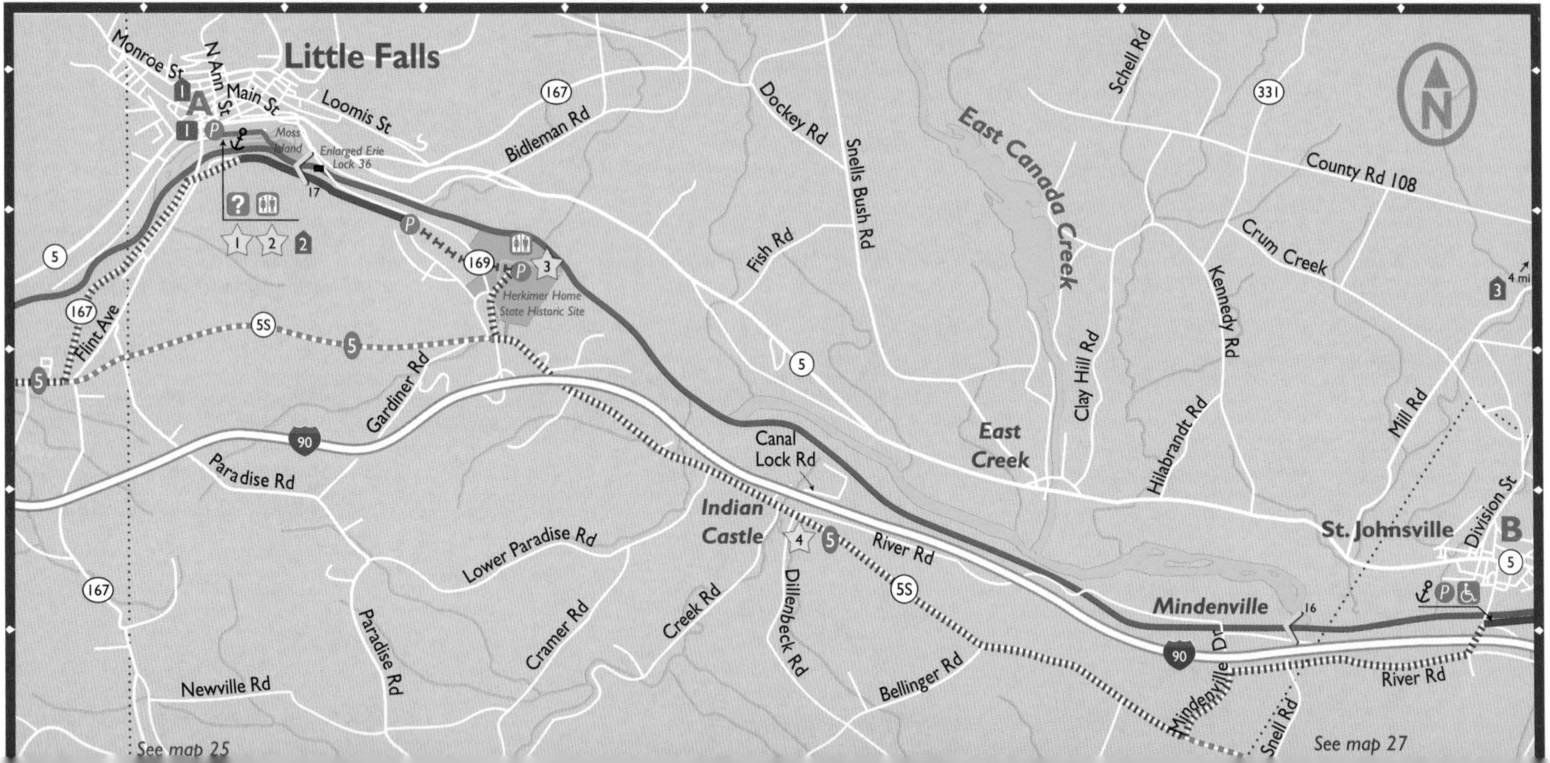

N

3 4 mi

Division St

5

B

River Rd

See map 27

Snell Rd

St. Johnsville

Mill Rd

County Rd 108

Crum Creek

331

Kennedy Rd

Hilabrandt Rd

Schell Rd

Mindenville

16

Minenville Dr

90

Clay Hill Rd

East Canada Creek

East Creek

Bellinger Rd

5S

River Rd

5

Snells Bush Rd

Dockey Rd

Fish Rd

5

Canal Lock Rd

4

5

3

Indian Castle

Dillenbeck Rd

Creek Rd

Little Falls

167

Bidleman Rd

Loomis St

Herkimer Home State Historic Site

P

169

3

P

Lower Paradise Rd

Cramer Rd

N Ann St

Main St

Monroe St

Moss Island

Enlarged Erie Lock 36

17

P

?

1 2

?

1 2 3

Gardiner Rd

5

Paradise Rd

90

Paradise Rd

Paradise Rd

5

5S

Newville Rd

See map 25

167

Flint Ave

5S

167

5

5

THINGS TO SEE & DO

1	Historic Canal Place	S Ann Street	(315) 823-1907
2	Little Falls Historical Society	319 S Ann Street	(315) 823-3014
3	Herkimer Home State Historic Site	200 Route 169	(315) 823-0398
4	Indian Castle Church	Route 5S	(518) 568-7779

Herkimer Home State Historic Site

TRAIL & TRAVEL NOTES

Location Drives Development — Situated within a deep gorge at the narrowest point in the Mohawk Valley, Little Falls first developed at the portage site around a difficult set of rapids. Before the Erie Canal was built, its predecessor, the 1792 Western Inland Canal, allowed river traffic to circumnavigate this obstacle. The success of the Western Inland Canal, which had a basic system of dams and locks, demonstrated the potential for a continuous canal to the Great Lakes.

Glacial Potholes — Adjacent to Lock 17, one of the highest lift locks in the world, is Moss Island, a National Natural Landmark known for fine examples of deep chimney potholes, formed in the bedrock by the scouring action of river stones in a rapid current.

Herkimer Home — Revolutionary War General Nicholas Herkimer led the defeat of the British at the Battle of Oriskany, considered a turning point in the war. Herkimer died soon after at his 1764 home, now a National Historic Landmark and State Historic Site dedicated to interpreting life in the Mohawk Valley during the Revolutionary War era.

Historic Canal Place

SERVICE AREAS

A $ ⑩ Rx ☂ 🍴 🛏 📷 ✈
B ⑪ Rx ☂ 🍴 🛏 ⚓

83

MAP 27 ST. JOHNSVILLE – CANAJOHARIE

84

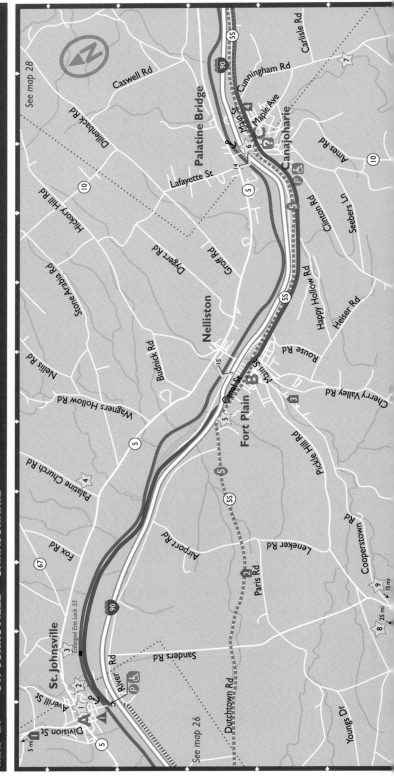

THINGS TO SEE & DO

1 Margaret Reaney Memorial Library & Museum	19 Kingsbury Avenue	(518) 568-7822
2 Fort Klock Historic Restoration	Route 5	(518) 568-7779
3 Nellis Tavern & Canal Locks Restoration	Route 5	(518) 568-2952
4 Palatine Church	Palatine Church Road	(518) 993-3539
5 Fort Plain Museum	389 Canal Street	(518) 993-2527
6 Canajoharie Library and Art Gallery	2 Erie Boulevard	(518) 673-2314
7 Canajoharie Gorge	Wintergreen Park Road	(518) 673-5512
8 National Baseball Hall of Fame - Cooperstown	25 Main Street	(607) 547-7201
9 Glimmerglass State Park	1527 County Hwy 31	(607) 547-8862

Canajoharie Library art collection

TRAIL & TRAVEL NOTES

German Settlers — Germans from the Palatine area of the Rhine River Valley came to America wishing to escape religious persecution and found in the Mohawk Valley a landscape similar to their homeland. In 1750, Palatine Johannes Klock built Fort Klock, a stone fur-trading post and privately-fortified dwelling, which served as a place of refuge during the French and Indian and Revolutionary Wars.

Family Business to National Brand — A family business, started in 1891 in Canajoharie, gave rise to the Beech-Nut Packing Company that produced a variety of food products. Beech-Nut entered the baby food business in 1931, creating a new industry standard by using clear glass jars. Baby food is the only product now made at the sprawling factory on the canal.

Cultural Gift to the Community — The Canajoharie Library and Art Gallery owes its existence to Bartlett Arkell, Beech-Nut's first president. The art gallery, founded in 1924, contains paintings and decorative arts acquired and donated by Arkell, most notably American landscapes and works by Winslow Homer.

Historic view of Beech-Nut plant

VISITOR INFORMATION

Canajoharie Information Kiosk
Canajoharie
Wagner Square

SERVICE AREAS

A
B $
C $

85

MAP 28   CANAJOHARIE – FULTONVILLE

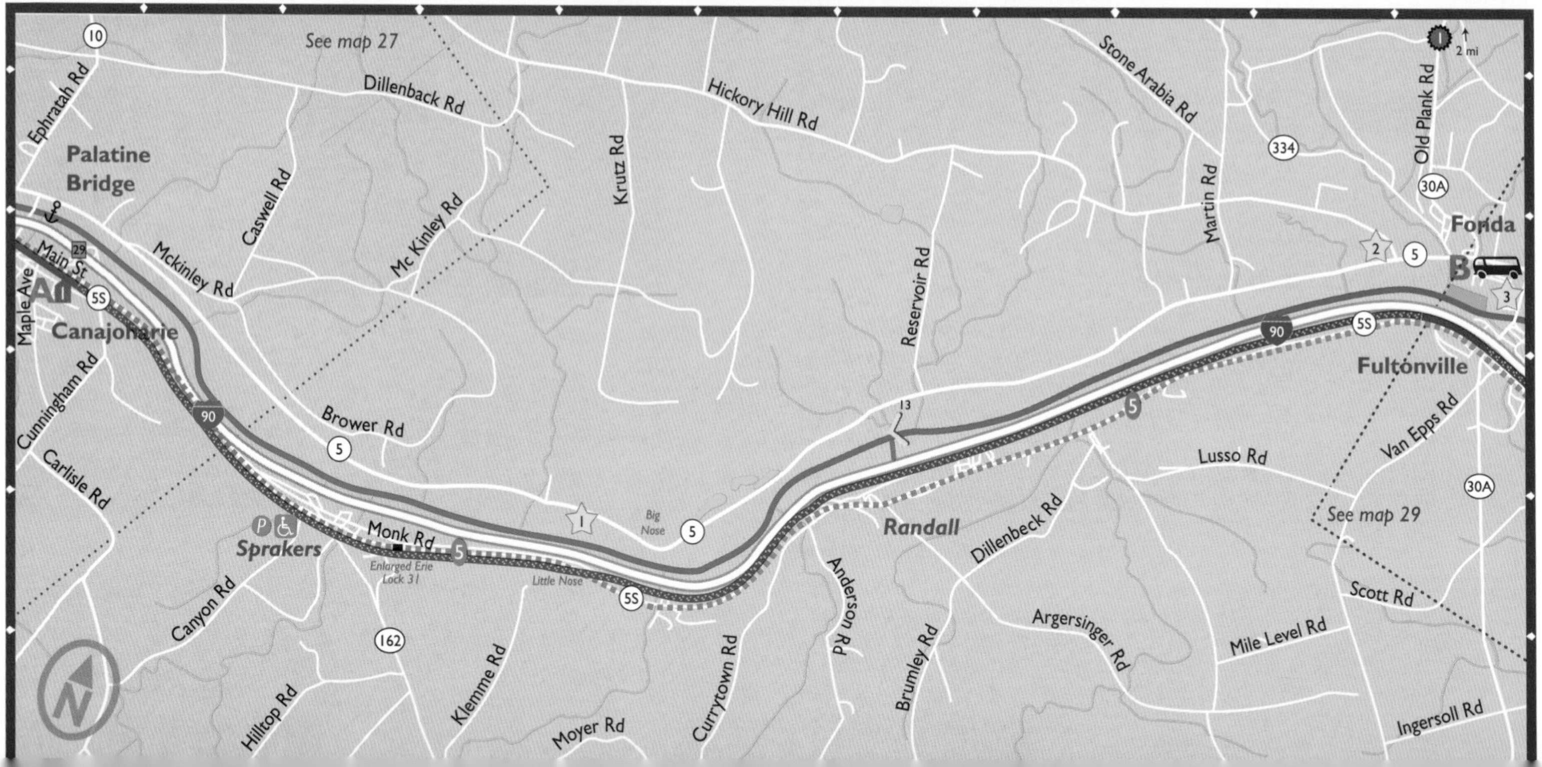

Old Plank Rd

Fonda

30A

30A

5

2

334

Martin Rd

Stone Arabia Rd

Fultonville

Van Epps Rd

5S

90

Lusso Rd

See map 29

Mile Level Rd

Scott Rd

Ingersoll Rd

5

Argersinger Rd

Dillenbeck Rd

Randall

Brumley Rd

Reservoir Rd

13

Anderson Rd

Hickory Hill Rd

Currytown Rd

5

Big Nose

5S

Kruzz Rd

1

Little Nose

Moyer Rd

Klemme Rd

Dillenback Rd

Mc Kinley Rd

See map 27

Brower Rd

5

Monk Rd

Enlarged Erie
Lock 3

5

162

Hilltop Rd

Caswell Rd

Sprakers

Canyon Rd

Mckinley Rd

Palatine
Bridge

10

Ephratah Rd

Cunningham Rd

Carlisle Rd

Maple Ave

Main St

5S

5

90

Canajoharie

2 mi

N

THINGS TO SEE & DO

1 Kanatsiohareke Mohawk Community	4934 State Route 5	(518) 673-5356
2 National Kateri Tekakwitha Shrine & Indian Museum	Route 5	(518) 853-3646
3 Fonda Speedway / Montgomery County Fairgrounds	21 S Bridge Street	(518) 382-3115

View of the Noses

TRAIL & TRAVEL NOTES

The Noses — The Mohawk River provides the only natural waterway through the Appalachian Mountain system between the St. Lawrence River and the Gulf of Mexico. A bit east of Sprakers, a spur of the Adirondacks forces the Mohawk River to bend and narrow, creating the area known as "the noses," as two steep escarpments face each other across the river. Watch for vultures, hawks, and the occasional bald eagle soaring on the updrafts created by winds deflecting off the cliffs.

Boating on the Canal — The 524-mile New York State Canal System includes the Champlain, Oswego, and Cayuga-Seneca Canals in addition to the Erie. Connecting with hundreds of miles of lake, river, and inland waterway, the Canal System operates from early May to early November. Cruise the canal on a guided excursion or charter a boat and explore the canals on your own. The canal also offers great canoeing and kayaking. For more information on boat hires, call 1-800-4canal4 or visit www.canals.state.ny.us/exvac.

Touring along the canal

SERVICE AREAS

A $ ⊙

B $ ⊙

Boating & biking go together on the canal

87

MAP 29 FULTONVILLE – AMSTERDAM

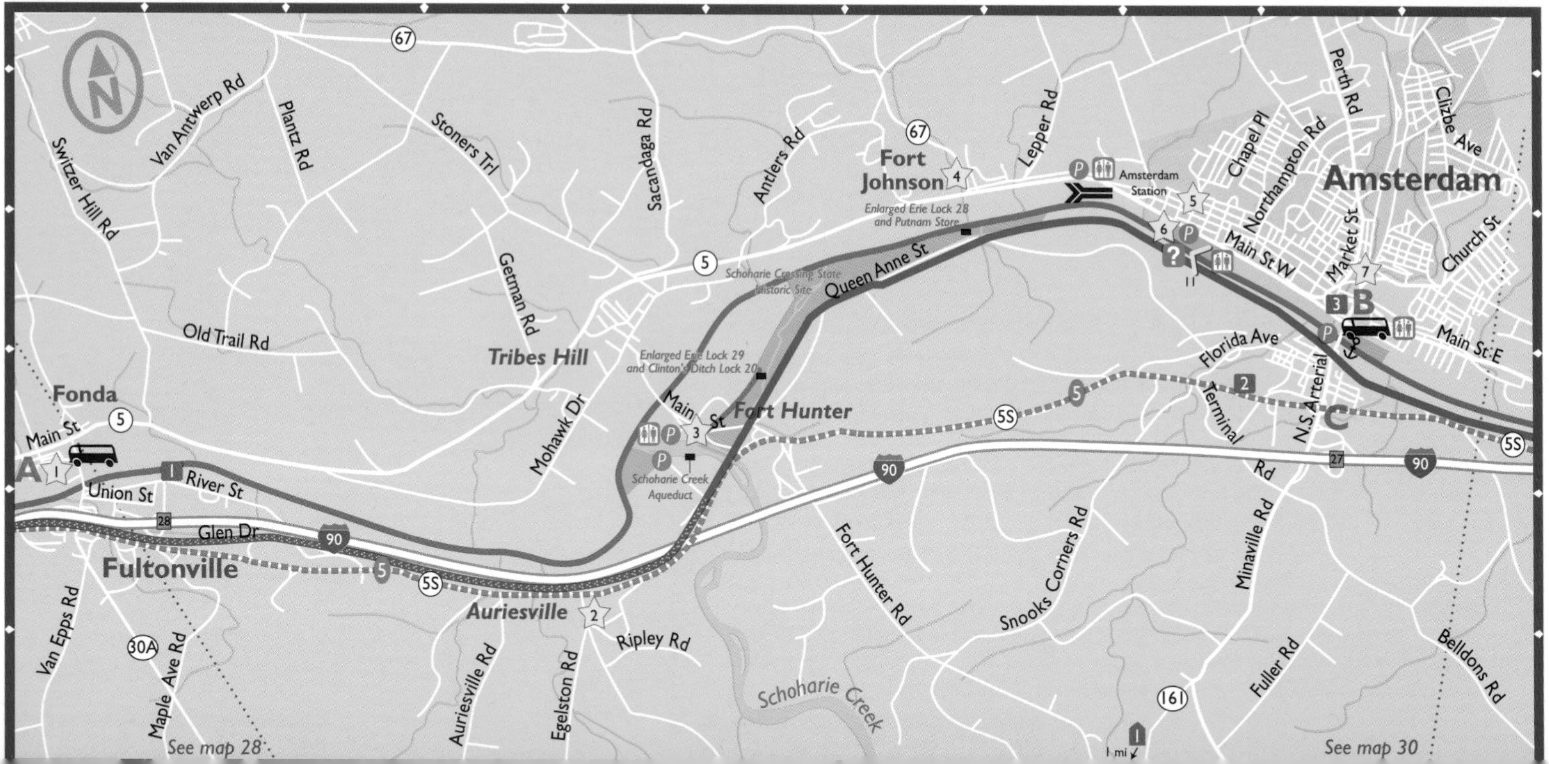

Amsterdam

Clizbe Ave

Perth Rd

Church St

Main St E

Market St

Main St W

Northampton Rd

Chapel Pl

Lepper Rd

Amsterdam Station

N.S. Arterial

Florida Ave

Terminal

Minaville Rd

Fuller Rd

Snooks Corners Rd

Belldons Rd

See map 30

Fort Johnson

Enlarged Erie Lock 28 and Putnam Store

Queen Anne St

Schoharie Crossing State Historic Site

Anders Rd

Sacandaga Rd

Fort Hunter

Enlarged Erie Lock 29 and Clinton–Dutch Lock 20½

Main St

Schoharie Creek Aqueduct

Mohawk Dr

Fort Hunter Rd

Schoharie Creek

Ripley Rd

Egelston Rd

Auriesville Rd

Auriesville

Tribes Hill

Getman Rd

Stoners Trl

Old Trail Rd

Plantz Rd

Van Antwerp Rd

Switzer Hill Rd

Fonda

Main St

Union St

River St

Glen Dr

Fultonville

Maple Ave Rd

Van Epps Rd

See map 28

N

1 mi

THINGS TO SEE & DO

1	Fonda Speedway / Montgomery County Fairgrounds	21 S Bridge Street	(518) 382-3115
2	National Shrine of North American Martyrs	Noeltner Road & Route 5S	(518) 853-3033
3	Schoharie Crossing State Historic Site	129 Schoharie Street	(518) 829-7516
4	Fort Johnson National Historic Site	Route 5 & Fort Johnson Avenue	(518) 843-0300
5	Walter Elwood Museum	300 Guy Park Avenue	(518) 843-5151
6	Guy Park Manor / Lock 11 Park	366 W Main Street	(518) 842-8200
7	Noteworthy Indian Museum	Corner of Church & Prospect St	(518) 843-4761

Schoharie Aqueduct

TRAIL & TRAVEL NOTES

Schoharie Crossing State Historic Site — The original Erie Canal, the four-foot-deep "Clinton's Ditch," was enlarged or relocated three times to accommodate bigger canal boats and cargo loads. Schoharie Crossing is the only place where you can see elements from all four iterations in one place. The most impressive canal structure here is the remains of Schoharie Aqueduct, originally 624 feet long, which carried the enlarged canal over Schoharie Creek.

National Shrine of North American Martyrs — The Auriesville Shrine, which honors the only canonized North American martyrs (including St. Isaac Jogues), is a major Roman Catholic pilgrimage site, with a round church that seats 6,500.

The "Rug City" — Perched on a steep hillside, Amsterdam's ample water-generated power and its proximity to the Erie Canal led to a burgeoning of textile industries, especially rug manufacturing. The hulking rug mills line the riverbank.

Cycling Tips — Within Schoharie Crossing State Historic Site, you can use either the paved bike path or the unpaved towpath.

Amsterdam Riverlink Park

VISITOR INFORMATION

Montgomery County Chamber of Commerce
Amsterdam • (518) 842-8200
366 W Main Street
www.montgomerycountyny.com

SERVICE AREAS

A	$	⏚	🍴	🛏	🏕	✉	⚒	⚓
B	$	⏚ Rx						⛴
C	$	⏚		⛽				

89

MAP 30 ROTTERDAM JUNCTION

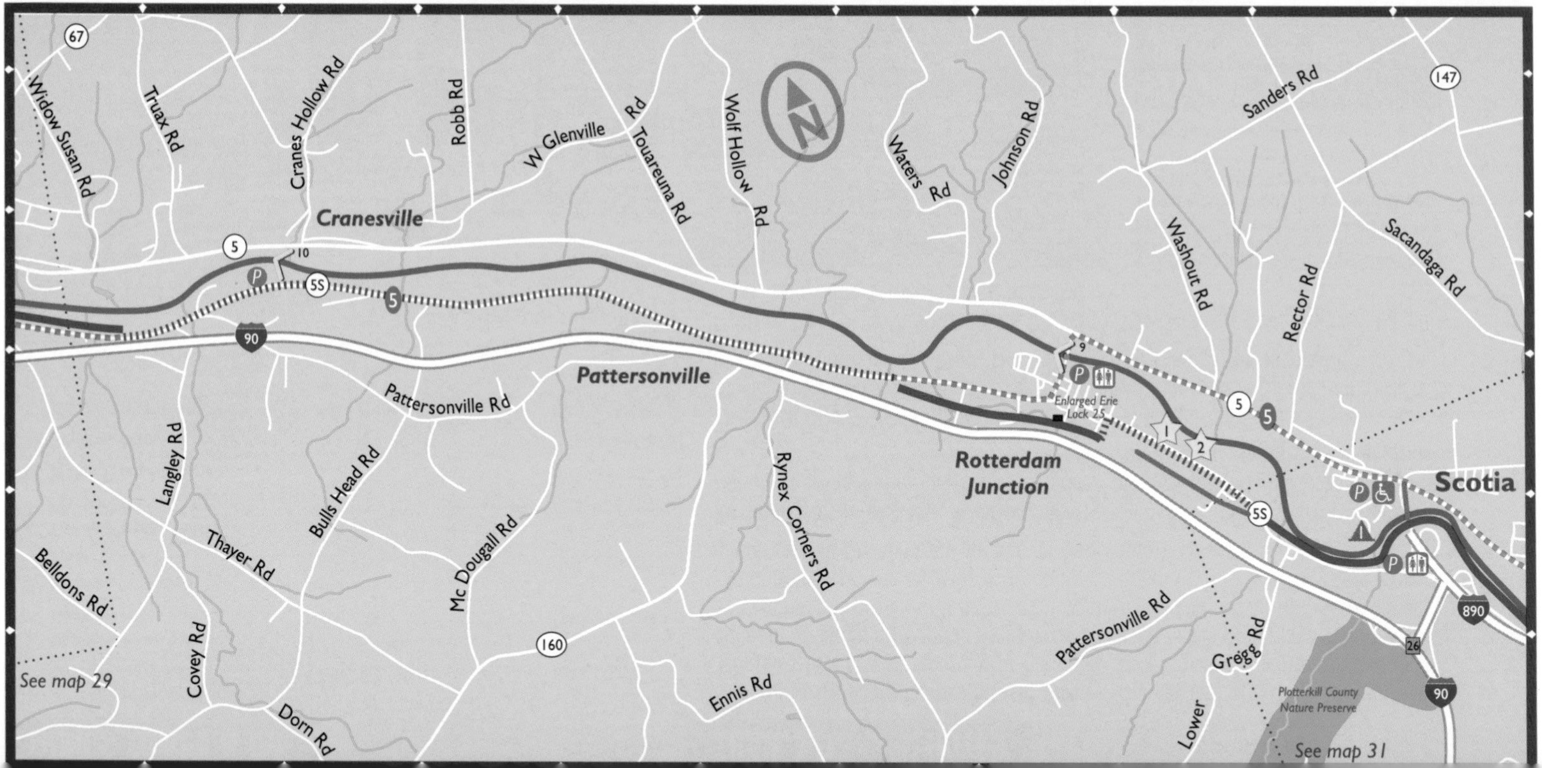

Scotia

890

90

26

55

5

5

147

Sacandaga Rd

Rector Rd

Sanders Rd

Washout Rd

Johnson Rd

Waters Rd

Wolf Hollow Rd

Touareuna Rd

W Glenville Rd

Robb Rd

Cranes Hollow Rd

Truax Rd

Widow Susan Rd

67

Enlarged Erie
Lock 23

1
2

9

Rotterdam
Junction

Rynex Corners Rd

Pattersonville

Pattersonville Rd

McDougall Rd

Bulls Head Rd

Thayer Rd

Langley Rd

Covey Rd

Dorn Rd

Belldons Rd

160

10

55

5

90

5

Patersonville Rd

Gregg Rd

Lower

Plotterkill County
Nature Preserve

See map 31

See map 29

P

P

P

P

THINGS TO SEE & DO

1	Keepers of the Circle Native American Center	1180 Main Street
2	Mabee Farm Historic Site	1080 Main Street

(518) 887-2590

(518) 887-5073

Mabee Farm homestead

TRAIL & TRAVEL NOTES

Mabee Farm — The Mabee Farm, owned by the same family for nearly 300 years, rests in a picture-perfect setting with a gorgeous view of the Mohawk Valley. The 1700 Dutch Colonial stone house is the oldest remaining Dutch farmhouse in the Mohawk Valley. The Schenectady County Historical Society manages the home and a re-created Dutch-style barn as a museum.

Fishing on the Canal — Fishing is popular on the canal and usually allowed at lock approach walls. Likely species include panfish, small mouth bass, perch, pike, pickerel, and, in some areas, trout and salmon. Anyone over 16 needs a NYS fishing license, available from most municipal clerks' offices and sporting goods stores or by calling 1-86-NY-DECALS.

Cycling Tips — The easternmost 35 miles of the Erie Canalway Trail follow the paved Mohawk-Hudson Bike-Hike Trail. An excellent detailed map of this part of the trail route is available from the Capital District Transportation Committee at (518) 458-2161.

Rollerbladers enjoy a paved section of the trail

Fort Johnson

MAP 31   SCHENECTADY

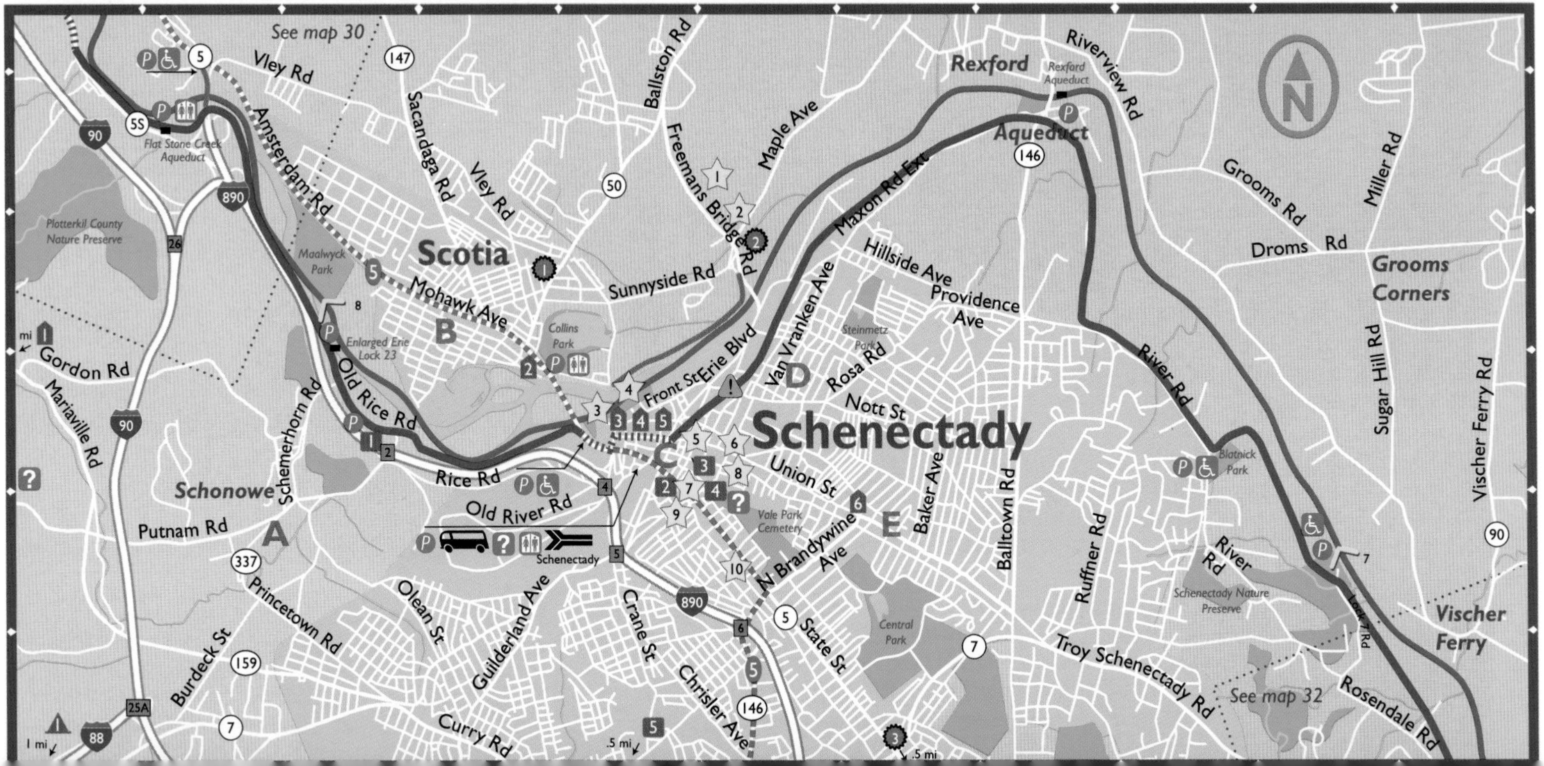

92

N

See map 30

Mariaville Rd

Gordon Rd

Plotterkill County Nature Preserve

Flat Stone Creek Aqueduct

88

25A

Burdeck St

7

159

Princetown Rd

337

Putnam Rd

Schonowee Rd

Amsterdam Rd

147

Vley Rd

Sacandaga Rd

Vley Rd

Scotia

Mohawk Ave

Collins Park

Enlarged Erie Lock 23

Mohawk Park

Old Rice Rd

Schemerhorn Rd

Schonowee Rd

A

Olean St

Curry Rd

Guilderland Ave

Crane St

State St

Chrisler Ave

Central Park

7

Schenectady

E

N Brandywine Ave

Union St

Vale Park Cemetery

Baker Ave

Ballstown Rd

D

Nott St

Rosa Rd

Steinmetz Park

Van Vranken Ave

Hillside Ave

Providence Ave

Maple Ave

Front St

Erie Blvd

Freemans Bridge Rd

Ballston Rd

Sunnyside Rd

Nixon Rd East

Rexford Aqueduct

Rexford

Aqueduct

146

Riverview Rd

River Rd

River Rd

Ruffner Rd

Troy Schenectady Rd

Schenectady Nature Preserve

River Rd

Bevswick Park

Lock 7 Rd

Sugar Hill Rd

Grooms Corners

Miller Rd

Droms Rd

Grooms Rd

Vischer Ferry Rd

Vischer Ferry

90

Rosendale Rd

See map 32

Old River Rd

Rice Rd

Schenectady

890

5

146

6

50

26

90

890

5S

5

B

C

147

THINGS TO SEE & DO

1	Glenville Mini Sportsplex	104 Freemans Bridge Road	(518) 393-4140
2	Indian Kill Preserve	Maple Avenue	(518) 386-2225
3	Schenectady County Historical Society	32 Washington Avenue	(518) 374-0263
4	Schenectady Stockade National Historic District	Front Street	(518) 374-0263
5	Professional Wrestling Hall of Fame	123 Broadway	(518) 785-5537
6	Union College & Mandeville Gallery	Union Street	(518) 388-6000
7	Jay Street Pedestrian Mall	Corner of Jay and State St	(518) 382-2663
8	Schenectady Museum	Nott Terrace Heights	(518) 382-7890
9	Proctor's Theatre	432 State Street	(518) 346-2604
10	Schenectady Light Opera Theater	826 State Street	(518) 393-5732

Trail at Train Station Park in Niskayuna

TRAIL & TRAVEL NOTES

The "Electric City" — Located in an area the Mohawk Indians called the "Great Flats," Schenectady was a natural gateway to the west. It became even more important as a commercial and transportation center with the coming of the Erie Canal. In 1886, Edison Machine Works set up shop to make electrical equipment. The company grew into the colossal General Electric Company of today, earning Schenectady the nickname of "Electric City."

Historic Stockade — Dutch settlers founded Schenectady in 1661. The Dutch influence is visible in much of the architecture of the historic Stockade District, which, according to the National Trust for Historic Preservation, has "more old buildings on their original sites than anywhere else in the U.S." More than 66 homes and buildings dating between 1700 and 1850 are found in the area around Front and Union Streets.

Cycling Tips — ⚠ The street-level trail crossing of Nott Street is very busy. The direct route through downtown from the Community College is R on State, L on Washington, R on Union, L on Jay to trailhead on R, but take some time to explore the Stockade District.

Nott Memorial at Union College

VISITOR INFORMATION

Chamber of Schenectady County
Schenectady • (518) 372-5656
306 State Street • www.schenectadychamber.org
Schenectady Heritage Area Visitors Center
Nott Terrace Heights • (518) 382-7890
www.schenectadynewyork.org

SERVICE AREAS

A	$	🏠						🔧
B	$	🏠	Rx	⚑	🍴	🏠	⛽	▷
C	$	🏠	Rx	⚑	🍴	🏠		🔧
D	$	🏠	Rx	⚑	🍴	🏠		▷
E	🏠	Rx	⚑	🍴	🏠			🛒

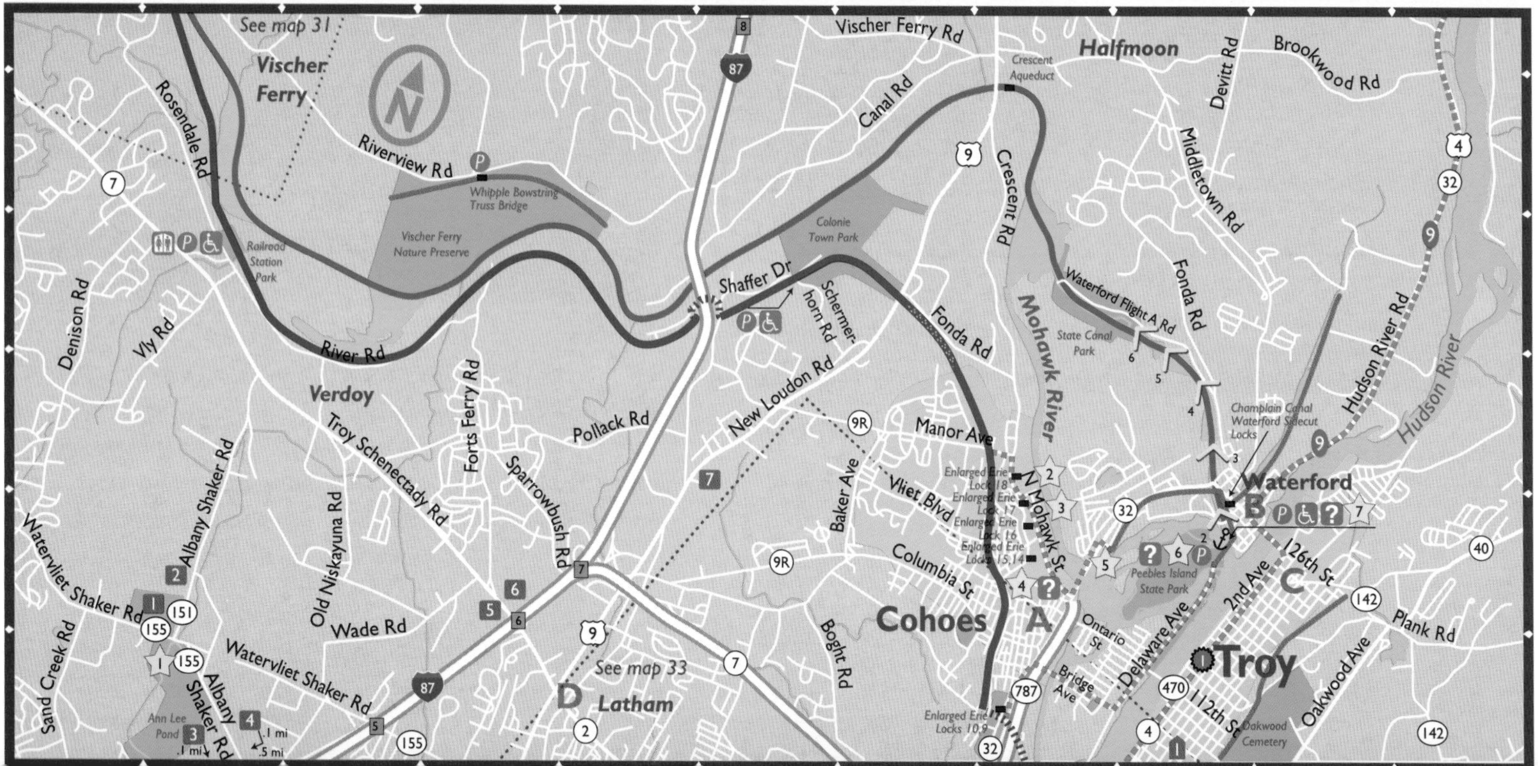

MAP 32   COHOES – WATERFORD

Brookwood Rd

Devitt Rd

Middletown Rd

Halfmoon

Fonda Rd

Hudson River Rd

Waterford

4
32
9

Hudson River

40

Plank Rd

142

Oakwood Ave

26th St

Troy

142

2nd Ave

Peebles Island
State Park

Champlain Canal
Waterford Sidecut
Locks

3

4

5

6

Waterford Flight A Rd

State Canal
Park

Mohawk River

32

5

Ontario St

Bridge Ave

787

C

12th St

Oakwood
Cemetery

470

4

32

Crescent
Aqueduct

9

Crescent Rd

Fonda Rd

Manor Ave

N 2

Mohawk St

3

Enlarged Erie
Lock 18

Enlarged Erie
Lock 17

Enlarged Erie
Lock 16

Vliet Blvd

Enlarged Erie
Lock 15

Columbia St

4

A

Enlarged Erie
Locks 10-6

32

Cohoes

Vischer Ferry Rd

Canal Rd

Colonie
Town Park

Schermer-
horn Rd

Shaffer Dr

New London Rd

Baker Ave

9R

9R

Boght Rd

7

8
87

Whipple Bowstring
Truss Bridge

Vischer
Ferry

See map 31

P

Riverview Rd

Vischer Ferry
Nature Preserve

River Rd

Railroad
Station Park

Rosendale Rd

Viv Rd

Denison Rd

7

Verdoy

Troy Schenectady Rd

Sparrowbush Rd

Forts Ferry Rd

Pollack Rd

7

7

See map 33

9

2

Latham D

6

5

6

5

87

155

Albany Shaker Rd

Watervliet Shaker Rd

Old Niskayuna Rd

Wade Rd

5

155

Ann Lee
Pond

3

4

1 mi

5 mi

Albany
Shaker Rd

Watervliet Shaker Rd

151

2

1

155

155

Sand Creek Rd

Watervliet Shaker Rd

THINGS TO SEE & DO

1 Shaker Heritage Society   Albany Shaker Road   **(518) 456-7890**

2 Cohoes Falls Overlook   School & Cataract Streets

3 Harmony Mills Complex   North Mohawk Street

4 Riverspark Visitor Center   58 Remsen Street   **(518) 237-7999**

5 Waterford Historical
   Society & Museum   2 Museum Lane   **(518) 238-0809**

6 Peebles Island State Park   Delaware Avenue off Ontario St   **(518) 237-8643**

6 Peebles Island & Erie Canalway
   National Heritage Corridor Visitor
   Center (opens 2005)   Delaware Avenue off Ontario St   **(518) 237-8643**

7 Waterford Harbor Visitor Center   1 Tugboat Alley   **(518) 233-9123**

Cohoes Falls

TRAIL & TRAVEL NOTES

Cohoes Falls — This 70-foot-high cataract is among the most powerful east of the Rockies and was a principal challenge for Erie Canal engineers, requiring many locks. Several fine examples of the Enlarged Erie lock structures are visible in Cohoes today.

Peebles Island State Park — Trails around the rocky cliffs of this 'channel island' give a unique perspective of the powerful erosive force of the Mohawk River at its confluence with the Hudson River. The park contains the remains of the Matton Shipyard, which built wooden canal boats and steel tugboats for use on the Erie and Champlain canals as well as Revolutionary War earthworks that were constructed to halt the British advance on Albany.

Harmony Mills — When built around the mid 19th century, these were the largest cotton textile mills in the world. The Mohawk's falling waters were diverted into a network of canals and sluiceways that powered the city's mill machinery through an intricate system of drive wheels, turbines, shafts, and belts. Examples of the worker housing built by the Harmony Company still stand near the mills.

VISITOR INFORMATION

Waterford Harbor Visitor Center
Waterford • (518) 233-9123
1 Tugboat Alley
http://town.waterford.ny.us/visitor_center.htm

**Peebles Island & Erie Canalway National
Heritage Corridor Visitor Center (opens 2005)**
Cohoes • (518) 237-8643
www.eriecanalway.org

RiverSpark Visitor Center
Cohoes • (518) 237-7999
58 Remsen Street
www.cohoes.com/abcohoes/rivspark.html

SERVICE AREAS

A $ ⑪ Rx ✈ 🍴 🛏 🔧 ⛟
B $ ⑪ 🍴 🛏 🔧 ⛟
C $ ⑪ Rx ✈ 🍴 🛒
D $ ⑪ Rx ✈ 🍴 🛏 ⛟ 🔧

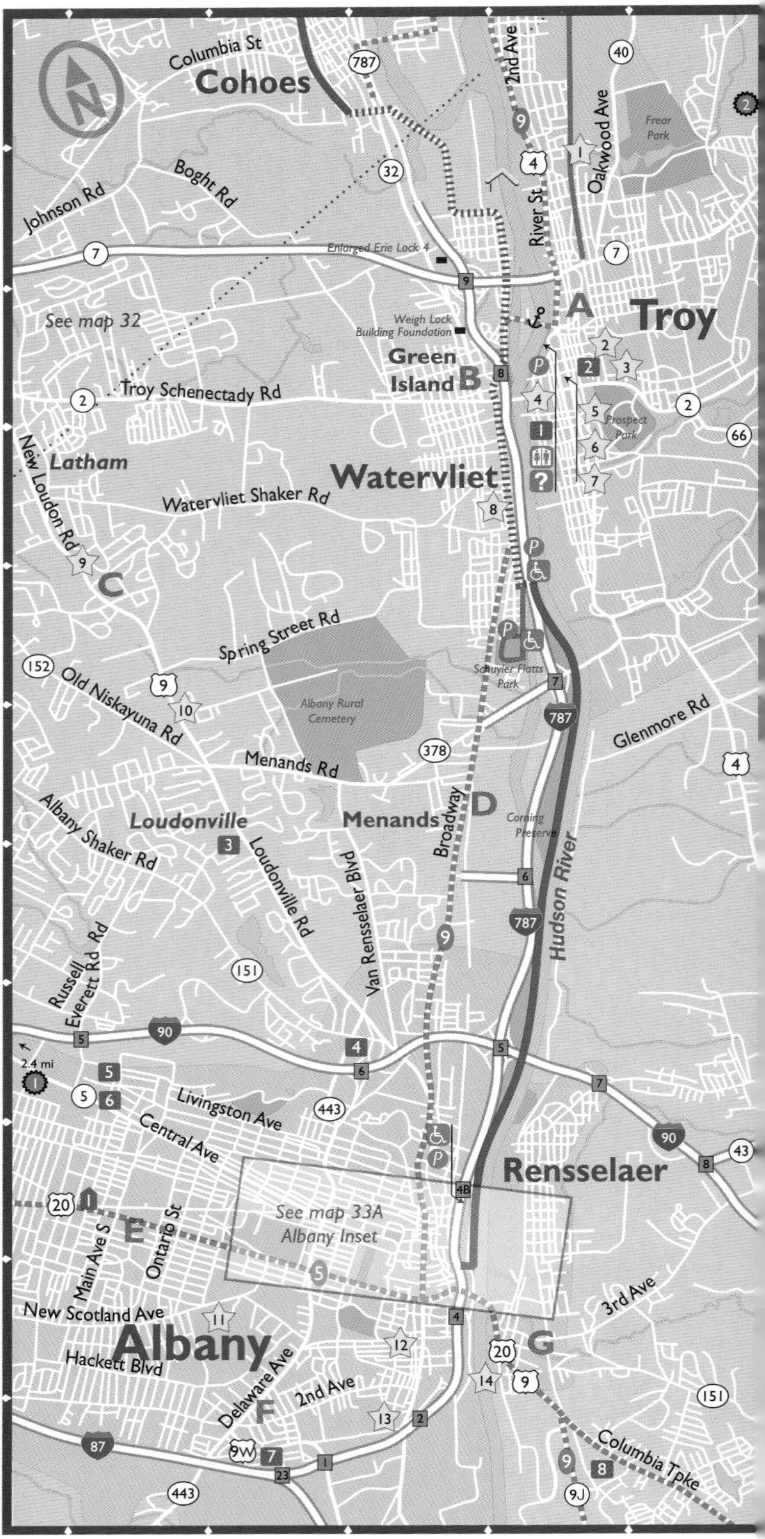

MAP 33   TROY – ALBANY

Columbia St

Cohoes

787

2nd Ave

40

9

Oakwood Ave

Frear Park

4

River St

Boght Rd

32

7

Johnson Rd

7

Enlarged Erie Lock 4

9

Troy

A

Troy Schenectady Rd

See map 32

Weigh Lock Building Foundation

Green Island

B

P

2

2

3

4

5

Prospect Park

2

66

New Loudon Rd

2

Latham

Watervliet

6

7

Watervliet Shaker Rd

8

9

C

Spring Street Rd

P

Schuyler Flatts Park

152

Old Niskayuna Rd

9

10

Albany Rural Cemetery

7

787

Glenmore Rd

4

Menands Rd

378

Albany Shaker Rd

Loudonville

3

Menands

D

Corning Preserve

Loudonville Rd

Broadway

Hudson River

151

Van Rensselaer Blvd

6

787

Russell Rd

Everett Rd

9

5

90

4

6

5

7

2.4 mi

5

5

6

Livingston Ave

443

5

Rensselaer

90

8

43

Central Ave

4B

20

1

E

Ontario St

See map 33A Albany Inset

5

Main Ave S

New Scotland Ave

11

Albany

4

20

G

3rd Ave

Hackett Blvd

Delaware Ave

12

14

9

151

2nd Ave

F

13

2

Columbia Tpke

87

9W

7

23

9

8

443

9J

THINGS TO SEE & DO

#	Name	Address	Phone
1	Oakwood Cemetery	Head of 101st Street	(518) 272-7520
2	The Junior Museum	105 8th Street	(518) 235-2120
3	Rensselaer Polytechnic Institute	110 8th Street	(518) 276-6000
4	Troy RiverSpark Heritage Area	251 River Street	(518) 270-8667
4	Captain JP Cruise Line	278 River Street	(518) 270-1901
5	Rensselaer County Historical Society	57 Second Street	(518) 272-7232
6	Troy Savings Bank Music Hall	32 Second Street	(518) 273-0038
7	Russell Sage College – Troy	45 Ferry Street	(518) 244-2000
8	Watervliet Arsenal – Museum of the Big Guns	Broadway & 3rd Avenue	(518) 266-5805
9	Hoffman's Playland	608 Loudon Road (Route 9)	(518) 785-3842
10	Siena College	515 Loudon Road (Route 9)	(518) 783-2300
11	Russell Sage College – Albany	140 New Scotland Avenue	(518) 244-2000
12	Schuyler Mansion State Historic Site	32 Catherine Street	(518) 434-0834
13	Historic Cherry Hill	523 S Pearl Street	(518) 434-4791
14	Crailo State Historic Site	9 Riverside Avenue	(518) 463-8738

TRAIL & TRAVEL NOTES

Wealth and Work — Ample waterpower and the twin 'water-level' canal and railroad transportation routes combined to make Cohoes and its neighbor, Troy, early leaders in the rise of industrial production. At one point Troy was one of the wealthiest cities in the nation, and this is reflected by its fine Victorian architecture. The hard work and low pay involved in laundering detachable shirt collars, which were invented here, inspired the formation of the first female labor union in the country.

State Capitol building

A Capital City — Albany succeeded several more southern Hudson River cities as the State Capital in 1797, owing to its location at the crossroads of the primary route between New York City and Montreal and the Great Lakes and western frontier. The city was originally established as a Dutch beaver pelt trading post, named Beverwyck. This Dutch heritage is still visible in the names, architecture, and traditions of the city.

River Street antiques district in Troy

VISITOR INFORMATION

RiverSpark Visitor Center
Troy • (518) 270-8667
251 River Street • www.troyvisitorcenter.org

SERVICE AREAS

A	$	⊕	Rx	🛒	👜	👕		✉	🔧
B	$	⊕	Rx	🛒		👕	🛒	✉	
C	$	⊕	Rx	🛒	👜	👕	🛒	✉	🔧
D	$	⊕		🛒		👕	🛒		
E	$	⊕	Rx	🛒	👜	👕	🛒	✉	🔧
F	$	⊕	Rx	🛒	👜	👕			
G	$	⊕	Rx	🛒		👕	🛒	✉	🔧

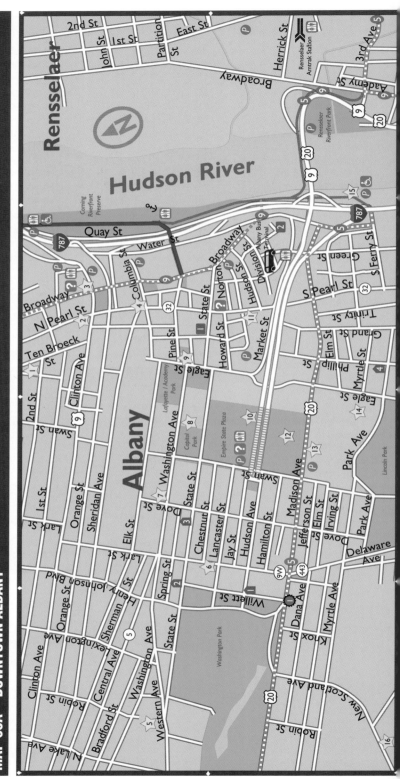

1	Ten Broeck Mansion	9 Ten Broeck Place	(518) 436-9826
2	Palace Theatre	N Pearl Street & Clinton Ave	(518) 465-4663
3	Albany Heritage Area Visitors Center & Henry Hudson Planetarium	25 Quackenbush Square	(518) 434-0405
3	Albany Aqua Ducks Amphibious Tours	Broadway at Quackenbush Square	(518) 462-3825
4	Capital Repertory Theatre	111 N Pearl Street	(518) 445-7469
5	SUNY Albany Downtown Campus & Paige Hall Theater	Western Avenue & State Street	(518) 442-3300
6	Lark Street Entertainment District	Washington Ave to Madison Ave	(518) 434-3861
7	Albany Institute of History and Art	125 Washington Avenue	(518) 463-4478
8	New York State Capitol	Washington Avenue and State St	(518) 474-2418
9	Albany City Hall	Eagle Street & Corning Place	(518) 434-5075
10	The Egg – State Performing Arts Center	Empire State Plaza	(518) 473-1061
11	Pepsi Arena	51 S Pearl Street	(518) 487-2000
12	Empire State Plaza Art Collection	Empire State Plaza & Concourse	(518) 474-2418
13	New York State Museum	Empire State Plaza & Madison Ave	(518) 474-5877
14	Executive Mansion	138 Eagle Street	(518) 473-7521
15	Destroyer U.S.S. Slater	Quay Street	(518) 431-1943
15	Dutch Apple Cruises	137 Broadway Avenue	(518) 463-0220
16	Albany Medical College	43 New Scotland Avenue	(518) 262-6008
16	Albany Law School	80 New Scotland Avenue	(518) 445-2311
16	Albany College of Pharmacy	106 New Scotland Avenue	(888) 203-8010

TRAIL & TRAVEL NOTES

State Capitol Building — Construction of this architecturally unique structure was completed in 1899 after nearly 30 years and a cost of $25 million. Several prominent architects contributed to its mix of styles, including Henry Hobson Richardson. The State Senate Chamber is one of the most ornate legislative chambers in the country, reflecting the style and symbolizing the wealth and prominence of New York State during the 'Gilded Age.' There are daily guided tours of the interior, which has been extensively restored to its historic grandeur.

Empire State Plaza — This huge international-style state office complex is an architectural feature itself, but also boasts an important collection of 20th century artwork, particularly sculpture. The New York State Museum at the opposite end of the public plaza from the Capitol features permanent exhibits about the Empire State's history and culture and hosts temporary fine art and cultural exhibits.

Empire State Plaza

VISITOR INFORMATION

Albany Convention & Visitors Bureau
25 Quackenbush Square • (518) 434-0405
www.albany.org/visitors

Empire State Plaza Info Center
Plaza Concourse • (518) 474-0549
www.ogs.state.ny.us/curatorial/plaza

I Love New York Visitor Information Center
330 South Pearl Street • (800) 225-5697

LODGING

MAP 1   BUFFALO SOUTH

B&B's / Inns / Hostels

1	Beau Fleuve B&B	242 Linwood Avenue	(716) 882-6116

Hotels / Motels

1	Buffalo Comfort Lodge	1159 Main Street	(716) 882-3490
2	Residence Inn	107 Anderson Road	(716) 893-8442
3	Hampton Inn - Airport Galleria	1745 Walden Avenue	(716) 894-8000
4	Sheraton	2040 Walden Avenue	(716) 681-2400
5	Homewood Suites	760 Dick Road	(716) 685-0700
6	Radisson Hotel Airport	4243 Genesee Street	(716) 634-2300
7	Quality Inn	4217 Genesee Street	(716) 633-5500
8	Days Inn	4345 Genesee Street	(716) 631-0800
9	Wellesley Inn	4630 Genesee Street	(716) 631-8966
10	Orchard Park Motel	3895 Broadway	(716) 674-6000

MAP 1A   DOWNTOWN BUFFALO

B&B's / Inns / Hostels

1	Betty's B&B	398 Jersey Street	(716) 881-0700
2	Richmond Place	45 Richmond Avenue	(716) 881-3242
3	HI - Buffalo Hostel	667 Main Street	(716) 852-5222

Hotels / Motels

1	Lenox Hotel & Suite	140 North Street	(716) 884-1700
2	Holiday Inn	620 Delaware Avenue	(716) 896-2900
3	Pillars Hotel	125 High Street	(716) 845-0112
4	Best Western Inn	510 Delaware Avenue	(716) 886-8333
5	Mansion on Delaware Avenue	414 Delaware Avenue	(716) 886-3300
6	Radisson Suites Downtown	601 Main Street	(716) 854-5500
7	Hampton Inn	220 Delaware Avenue	(716) 855-2223
8	Chippewa Hotel	47 West Chippewa Street	(716) 845-5413
9	Hyatt Regency	2 Fountain Plaza	(716) 856-1234
10	Adam's Mark Hotel	120 Church Street	(716) 845-5100

MAP 2   BUFFALO NORTH

B&B's / Inns / Hostels

1	Beau Fleuve B&B	242 Linwood Avenue	(716) 882-6116

Hotels / Motels

1	Grand Island Holiday Inn	100 Whitehaven Road	(716) 773-1111
2	Super 8 Motel	1288 Sheridan Drive	(716) 876-4020
3	Modern Aire Motel	1346 Sheridan Drive	(716) 876-4489
4	Buffalo Comfort Lodge	1159 Main Street	(716) 882-3490

MAP 3   TONAWANDAS

Hotels / Motels

1	Gateway Motel	2994 Niagara Falls Boulevard	(716) 693-4232
2	Royal Motel	3333 Niagara Falls Boulevard	(716) 693-5695
4	B-Cozy Motel	1200 Niagara Falls Boulevard	(716) 695-3437
3	Hayat Motel	1182 Niagara Falls Boulevard	(716) 694-0360

5	Esquire Motel	3930 Niagara Falls Boulevard	(716) 692-4222
6	Ellicott Park Court Motel	2740 Niagara Falls Boulevard	(716) 693-6412
7	Tuckett Inn	2436 Niagara Falls Boulevard	(716) 693-5533
8	Boulevard Gardens Court Motel	2424 Niagara Falls Boulevard	(716) 692-3842
9	White Horse Motel	2270 Niagara Falls Boulevard	(716) 693-2732
9	Blue Falls Motel	2142 Niagara Falls Boulevard	(716) 695-0433
9	Grand Motor Inn	2000 Niagara Falls Boulevard	(716) 694-6696
9	Amton Motel	1970 Niagara Falls Boulevard	(716) 692-7260
9	Boulevard Inn	1900 Niagara Falls Boulevard	(716) 692-1422
9	Royal Inn	1378 Niagara Falls Boulevard	(716) 836-2940

Campgrounds

| 1 | Donald F. Miller Memorial Park | 1601 Sweeney Street | (716) 743-0320 |
| 2 | Royal Campground | 3333 Niagara Falls Boulevard | (716) 693-5695 |

MAP 4   LOCKPORT

B&B's / Inns / Hostels

1	Deflippo's Inn	326 West Avenue	(716) 433-2913
2	Hambleton House	130 Pine Street	(716) 439-9507
3	Cottage Country BB	7745 Rochester Road	(716) 772-2251

Hotels / Motels

1	Lockport Motel	315 South Transit Street	(716) 434-5595
2	Holiday Inn	515 South Transit Street	(716) 434-6151
3	Comfort Inn	551 South Transit Street	(716) 434-4411
4	Hartland Motel	8464 Ridge Road	(716) 772-2266

Campgrounds

| 1 | Niagara County Camping Resort | 7369 Wheeler Road | (716) 434-3991 |

MAP 5   GASPORT-MEDINA

B&B's / Inns / Hostels

1	Canal Country Inn	4021 Peet Street	(716) 735-7572
2	Medina Stone Farm B&B	255 N. Gravel Road	(585) 798-9238
3	Garden View B&B	11091 West Center Street Ext.	(585) 798-1087
4	Victorian B&B	421 West Center Street	(716) 798-4595
5	Olde Victorian B&B	322 Park Avenue	(716) 798-4124

Hotels / Motels

| 1 | Hartland Motel | 8464 Ridge Road | (716) 772-2266 |
| 2 | Dollinger's Courtyard | 11360 Maple Ridge Road | (585) 798-0016 |

Campgrounds

| 1 | Middleport Boater/ Biker/Hiker Campsite | Village Canal Park | (716) 735-3303 |

MAP 6   MEDINA-ALBION

B&B's / Inns / Hostels

1	Medina Stone Farm B&B	255 N Gravel Road	(585) 798-9238
2	Garden View B&B	11091 West Center Street	(585) 798-1087
3	Victorian B&B	421 West Center Street	(716) 798-4595
4	Olde Victorian B&B	322 Park Avenue	(716) 798-4124

Hotels / Motels

1	Dollinger's Courtyard	11360 Maple Ridge Road	(585) 798-0016
2	Dollinger's Motor Inn	436 West Avenue	(585) 589-6308

MAP 7   ALBION-HOLLEY

B&B's / Inns / Hostels

1	Fair Haven Inn	14359 Ridge Road	(585) 589-9151
2	Lamont's Orchard View B&B	3027 Densmore Road	(585) 589-7702
3	Friendship Manor B&B	349 South Main Street	(585) 589-2983

Hotels / Motels

1	Gurney's Olde Coach Inn	35 North Main Street	(585) 589-9744
2	Dollinger's Motor Inn	436 West Avenue	(585) 589-6308
3	Dollinger's Motel	215 South Main Street	(585) 589-6308
4	Hotel Holley	1 Thomas Street	(585) 638-6460

Campgrounds

1	Holley Boater/Biker/ Hiker Campsite	Holley Canal Port	(585) 638-6567

MAP 8   BROCKPORT-SPENCERPORT

B&B's / Inns / Hostels

1	Portico B&B	3741 Lake Road North	(585) 637-0220
2	Trestle Inn	177 Utica Street	(585) 395-0676
3	Victorian B&B	320 Main Street	(585) 637-7519
4	B&B At The White	854 White Road	(585) 637-0459
5	Adams Basin Inn	425 Washington Street	(888) 352-3999

Hotels / Motels

1	Econo Lodge	6575 Fourth Section Road	(585) 637-3157
2	Holiday Inn Express	4908 Lake Road South	(585) 395-1000

MAP 9   ROCHESTER WEST

Hotels / Motels

1	Friendly Motel	4670 West Ridge Road	(585) 352-3785
2	Budget Inn	4671 West Ridge Road	(585) 349-3999
3	Comfort Inn	1501 West Ridge Road	(585) 621-5700
3	Courtyard by Marriott	400 Paddy Creek Circle	(585) 621-6050
3	Extended Stay America	600 Center Place Drive	(585) 663-5558
3	Hampton Inn	500 Center Place Drive	(585) 663-6070
3	Marriott - Residence Inn	500 Paddy Creek Circle	(585) 865-2090
3	Marriott Hotels & Resorts	1890 Ridge Road West	(585) 225-6880
3	Wellesley Inn - Greece	1635 Ridge Road West	(585) 621-2060
4	Best Western Inn	1956 Lyell Avenue	(585) 254-1000
5	490 Motel	360 Mount Read Boulevard	(585) 235-1139
6	Gates Motel	995 Buffalo Road	(585) 328-0550
7	Motel 6	155 Buell Road	(585) 436-2170
8	Fairfield Inn - Marriott	1200 Brooks Avenue	(585) 529-5000
9	Comfort Inn	395 Buell Road	(585) 436-4400
10	Holiday Inn	911 Brooks Avenue	(585) 328-6000

MAP 9A   DOWNTOWN ROCHESTER

B&B's / Inns / Hostels

1	The Inn on Broadway	26 Broadway	(585) 232-3595
2	Dartmouth House	215 Dartmouth Street	(585) 271-7872

Hotels / Motels

1	Crowne Plaza	70 State Street	(585) 546-3450
2	Four Points Hotel by Sheraton	120 Main Street East	(585) 546-6400
3	Hyatt Hotels & Resorts	125 Main Street East	(585) 546-1234
4	Extended Stay America	360 East Avenue	(585) 454-7755
5	Days Inn	384 East Avenue	(585) 325-5010
6	Strathallan	550 East Avenue	(585) 461-5010

MAP 10   ROCHESTER EAST

B&B's / Inns / Hostels

1	428 Mt. Vernon	428 Mount Vernon Avenue	(585) 271-0792
2	Edward Harris House B&B / Inn	35 Argyle Street	(585) 473-9752
3	Canal Lamp Inn	27 North Main Street	(585) 381-4351
4	Twenty Woodlawn B&B	20 Woodlawn Avenue	(585) 377-8224

Hotels / Motels

1	Dorkat Motel	3990 West Henrietta Road	(585) 334-7000
2	Courtyard by Marriott	33 Corporate Woods	(585) 292-1000
3	Hampton Inn	717 East Henrietta Road	(585) 272-7800
4	Wellesley Inn Brighton	797 East Henrietta Road	(585) 427-0130
5	Econo Lodge	940 Jefferson Road	(585) 427-2700
5	Extended Stay America	700 Commons Way	(585) 427-7580
5	Holiday Inn	1111 Jefferson Road	(585) 475-1510
5	Ramada Inn	800 Jefferson Road	(585) 475-9190
5	Residence Inn	1300 Jefferson Road	(585) 272-8850
6	Towpath Motel	2323 Monroe Avenue	(585) 271-2147
7	Aloha Motel	2729 Monroe Avenue	(585) 473-0310
8	Del Monte Lodge - Marriott	41 North Main Street	(585) 381-9900
9	Brookwood Inn	800 Pittsford-Victor Road	(585) 248-9000

MAP 11   FAIRPORT-PALMYRA

B&B's / Inns / Hostels

1	Esten-Wahl Farm B&B	4394 Carter Road	(585) 388-1881
2	Woods Edge B&B	151 Bluhm Road	(716) 223-8877

Hotels / Motels

1	Budget Inn	7340 Pittsford-Palmyra Road	(585) 223-1710
2	Wayne Villa Motel	334 Pittsford-Palmyra Road	(315) 986-5530

Campgrounds

1	Macedon Boater/ Biker/Hiker Campsite	Lock 30 Canal Park	(315) 986-5631

MAP 12   PALMYRA-NEWARK

B&B's / Inns / Hostels

1	Liberty House B&B	131 West Main Street	(315) 597-0011
2	Canaltown B&B	119 Canandaigua Street	(315) 597-5553
3	Thomas Galloway House at Paragon Farm	993 Cornwall Road	(315) 597-6742
4	Mil-Benski Farm B&B	6769 Miller Road	(315) 331-2798

Hotels / Motels

1	Quality Inn	125 North Main Street	(315) 331-9500

MAP 13   LYONS-CLYDE

B&B's / Inns / Hostels

1	Peppermint Cottage B&B	336 Pleasant Valley Road	(315) 946-4811
2	Roselawne B&B	101 Broad Street	(315) 946-4218

Campgrounds

1	Nor-Win Farm & Campsite	2921 Pilgrimport Road	(315) 946-4436

MAP 14   MONTEZUMA MARSH

Campgrounds

1	Oak Orchard Campsite	State Route 89 at Mays Point	(315) 365-3000
2	Hejamada Camping Resort	764 McDonald Road	(315) 776-5887

MAP 15   WATERLOO-SENECA FALLS

B&B's / Inns / Hostels

1	Through the Grapevine B&B	108 Virginia Street	(315) 539-8620
2	Hubbell House B&B	42 Cayuga Street	(315) 568-9690
3	Barristers B&B	56 Cayuga Street	(800) 914-0145
4	VanCleef Homestead B&B	86 Cayuga Street	(315) 568-2275
5	John Morris Manor	2138 Route 89	(315) 568-9057

Hotels / Motels

1	Waterloo Motel	989 Waterloo-Geneva Road	(315) 539-8042
2	Inland Motel	984 Waterloo-Geneva Road	(315) 539-0604
3	Holiday Inn	2468 State Route 414	(315) 539-5011
4	Chamberlain Mansion Hotel	30 Cayuga Street	(315) 568-9990
5	Starlite Motel	101 State Route 5/20	(315) 568-6149
6	Microtel Inn & Suites	1966 State Route 5/20	(888) 771-7171

Campgrounds

1	Hidden Harbor Campgrounds	1076 State Route 5/20	(315) 539-8034
2	Waterloo Harbor Campground	1278 State Route 5/20	(315) 539-8848
3	Cayuga Lake State Park	2678 Lower Lake Road	(315) 568-5163
4	Cayuga Lake Campground	2546 State Route 89	(315) 568-0919
5	Cayuga Marina & Campground	River Road	(315) 252-5754
6	Twin Oaks Campground	Lake Road	(315) 889-5189

MAP 16   PORT BYRON-WEEDSPORT

B&B's / Inns / Hostels

1	Lavender Patch Retreat B&B	8613 Denman Road	(315) 776-8632

Hotels / Motels

1	Best Western Weedsport Inn	2709 Erie Drive - Route 31	(315) 834-6623
2	Days Inn Weedsport	2731 Erie Drive - Route 31/34	(315) 834-6198

Campgrounds

1	Eagle Bay Campground & Marina	River Road	(315) 776-8648
2	Riverforest Park Campground	9439 Riverforest Road	(315) 834-9458

MAP 17   JORDAN-CAMILLUS

Hotels / Motels

1	Elbridge Motel	1067 State Route 5	(315) 689-3955
2	Cambridge Inn	2382 W Genesee Turnpike	(315) 672-3022
3	Motel Thomas	2100 State Route 5 W	(315) 672-3441

Campgrounds

1	Sunset Park	455 Sprague Road	(315) 635-6450

MAP 18   SYRACUSE WEST

B&B's / Inns / Hostels

1	Ancestors Inn at the Bassett House	215 Sycamore	(315) 461-1226
2	Dickenson House on James	1504 James Street	(315) 423-4777

Hotels / Motels

1	Western Ranch Motor Inn	1255 State Fair Boulevard	(315) 457-9236
2	Best Western - Fairgrounds	670 State Fair Boulevard	(315) 484-0044
3	LeMoyne Manor Inn	629 Old Liverpool Road	(315) 457-1240
4	Holiday Inn - Airport	441 Electronics Parkway	(315) 457-1122
5	Knights Inn Syracuse	430 Electronics Parkway	(315) 453-6330
6	Doubletree Club	6701 Buckley Road	(315) 457-4000
7	Ramada Inn	1305 Buckley Road	(315) 457-8670
8	Quality Inn	1308 Buckley Road	(315) 451-1212
9	Super 8 Motel - Airport	421 7th North Street	(315) 451-8888
10	Hampton Inn - Airport	417 7th North Street	(315) 457-9900
11	Econo Lodge - Liverpool	401 7th North Street	(315) 451-6000
12	Red Carpet Inn	2914 Brewerton Road	(315) 454-3266

MAP 18A   DOWNTOWN SYRACUSE

B&B's / Inns / Hostels

1	B&B Wellington	707 Danforth Street	(315) 474-3641

Hotels / Motels

1	Econo Lodge - University	454 James Street	(315) 425-0015
2	The Marx	701 E Genesee Street	(315) 479-7000
3	Genesee Inn Hotel	1060 E Genesee Street	(315) 476-4212
4	Sheraton University Hotel	801 University Avenue	(315) 475-3000
5	Hawthorn Suites - Armory Square	416 S Clinton Street	(315) 425-0500

MAP 19   SYRACUSE EAST

B&B's / Inns / Hostels

1	Beard Morgan House B&B	126 E Genessee Street	(315) 637-4234

Hotels / Motels
The following listings numbered "1" are in the Carrier Circle vicinity

1	Days Inn - Syracuse East	6609 Thompson Road	(315) 437-5998
1	Red Roof Inn	6614 Thompson Road	(315) 437-7865
1	Ramada Limited	6590 Thompson Road	(315) 463-0202
1	Comfort Inn	6491 Thompson Road	(315) 437-0222
1	Super 8 Motel East Syracuse	6620 Old Collamer Road	(315) 432-5612
1	Residence Inn by Marriot	6420 Yorktown Circle	(315) 432-4488
1	Extended Stay America	6630 Old Collamer Road	(315) 463-1958
1	CrestHill Suites	6410 New Venture Gear Drive	(315) 432-5595
1	Fairfield Inn	6611 Old Collamer Road	(315) 432-9333
1	Hampton Inn	6605 Old Collamer Road	(315) 463-6443
1	Holiday Inn Carrier Circle	6555 Old Collamer Road S	(315) 437-2761
1	Wyndham Syracuse	6301 Rte 298 / Carrier Parkway	(315) 432-0200
1	Embassy Suites Hotel	6646 Old Collamer Road	(315) 446-3200
1	Microtel	6608 Old Collamer Road	(315) 437-3500
1	Courtyard by Marriott	6415 Yorktown Circle	(315) 432-0300

1	Hilton Garden Inn	6004 Fair Lakes Road	(315) 431-4800
2	Dewitt Econo Lodge	3406 Erie Boulevard E	(315) 446-3300
3	Duboise Budget Motel	6864 E Genessee Street	(315) 446-1910
4	Craftsman Inn	7300 E Genessee Street	(800) 797-4464

Campgrounds

| 1 | Green Lakes State Park | 7900 Green Lakes Road | (315) 637-6111 |

MAP 20 CHITTENANGO-CANASTOTA

Hotels / Motels

1	Canastota Days Inn	377 N Peterboro Street	(315) 697-3309
2	Graziano's Motor Lodge	409 N Peterboro Street	(315) 697-8384
3	Sharway Motel	3669 Seneca Turnpike	(315) 697-7935

Campgrounds

| 1 | Chittenango Falls State Park | 2300 Rathbun Road | (315) 655-9620 |

MAP 21 ONEIDA

B&B's / Inns / Hostels

| 1 | Governor's House B&B | 50 Seneca Avenue | (315) 363-5643 |
| 2 | Charlotte's Creekside Inn B&B | 3960 Sconondoa Road | (315) 363-3377 |

Hotels / Motels

| 1 | Super 8 Motel | 215 Genesee Street | (315) 363-5168 |

Campgrounds

1	Verona Beach State Park	State Route 13	(315) 762-4463
2	Paradise Cove	Cove Rd & Erie Canal	(315) 762-0210
3	Ta-Ga Soke Campground	7820 Higginsville Road	(800) 831-1744
4	KOA Rome - Verona	6591 Blackmans Corners Road	(315) 336-7318

MAP 22 ROME

B&B's / Inns / Hostels

1	Maplecrest B&B	6480 Williams Road	(315) 337-0070
2	Angels Nest B&B	404 S George Street	(315) 334-4618
3	The Little Schoolhouse	6905 Dix Road	(315) 336-4474

Hotels / Motels

1	Rome Motel	8257 Turin Road	(315) 336-4200
2	Inn at the Beaches	7900 Turin Road	(315) 336-1776
3	Quality Inn of Rome	200 S James Street	(315) 336-4300
4	Travel Inn	145 E Whitesboro Street	(315) 337-9400
5	Red Carpet Inn	799 Lower Lawrence Avenue	(315) 339-3610
6	Adirondack 13 Pines Motel	7353 River Road	(315) 337-4930

Campgrounds

| 1 | KOA Rome - Verona | 6591 Blackmans Corners Road | (315) 336-7318 |
| 2 | Delta Lake State Park | 8797 Rte 46 | (315) 337-4670 |

MAP 23 ORISKANY

Hotels / Motels

| 1 | Airport Inn | 5920 Airport Road | (315) 736-3377 |
| 2 | Holiday Inn | 1777 Burrstone Road | (315) 797-2131 |

MAP 24   UTICA-FRANKFORT

B&B's / Inns / Hostels

1	Pratt Smith House	10497 Cosby Manor Road	(315) 732-8483
2	Rosemont Inn	1423 Genesee Street	(315) 792-8852
3	Iris Stonehouse B&B	16 Derbyshire Place	(315) 732-6720

Hotels / Motels

1	Country Motel	1477 Herkimer Road	(315) 732-4628
2	Super 8 Motel	309 N Genesee Street	(315) 797-0964
3	Happy Journey Hotel	300 N Genessee Street	(315) 738-1959
4	Best Western Gateway Adirondack	175 N Genessee Street	(315) 732-4121
5	A-1 Motel	238 N Genessee Street	(315) 735-6698
6	Hotel Utica	102 Lafayette Street	(315) 724-7829
7	Radisson Hotel-Utica Center	200 Genessee Street	(315) 797-8010

Campgrounds

| 1 | Elmtree Campsites | 2842 State Route 5 | (315) 724-6678 |

MAP 25   ILION-HERKMIER

B&B's / Inns / Hostels

1	Whiffletree Inn	345 East Main Street	(315) 895-7777
2	Bellinger Rose B&B	611 W German Street	(315) 867-2197
3	Putnam Manor House	112 West German Street	(315) 866-6738
4	Portobello Inn	5989 State Route 5	(315) 823-8612

Hotels / Motels

1	The Prospect Inn	200 Prospect Street	(315) 866-4400
2	Inn Towne Motel	227 N Washinton Street	(315) 866-1101
3	Herkimer Motel	100 Marginal Road	(315) 866-0490

Campgrounds

| 1 | Herkimer Diamond KOA | 5661 State Route 5 | (315) 891-7355 |

MAP 26   LITTLE FALLS-ST.JOHNSVILLE

B&B's / Inns / Hostels

1	Gansevoort House Inn	42 West Gansevoort Street	(315) 823-1833
2	Canalside Inn	395 South Ann Street	(315) 823-1170
3	Inn by the Mill	1679 Mill Road	(518) 568-2388

Hotels / Motels

| 1 | Best Western Little Falls Motor Inn | 20 Albany Street | (315) 823-4954 |

MAP 27   ST. JOHNSVILLE-CANAJOHARIE

B&B's / Inns / Hostels

1	Inn by the Mill	1679 Mill Road	(518) 568-2388
2	Hazelnut Farm B&B	205 Paris Road	(518) 993-3346
3	A White Rose B&B	105 Reid Street	(518) 993-3339
4	Window Box Guest House	23 Front Street	(518) 673-3131

Campgrounds

| 1 | St Johnsville Campsite | Marina Dr & Bridge Street | (518) 568-7406 |

MAP 28   CANAJOHARIE-FULTONVILLE

B&B's / Inns / Hostels
1   Window Box Guest House   23 Front Street   (518) 673-3131

MAP 29   FULTONVILLE-AMSTERDAM

B&B's / Inns / Hostels
1   Halcyon Farm B&B   Lang Road   (518) 842-7718

Hotels / Motels
1   Travelodge   123 Riverside Drive   (518) 853-4511
2   Valley View Motor Inn   1351 State Rte 5S   (518) 842-5637
3   Best Western   10 Market State   (518) 843-5760

MAP 30   ROTTERDAM JUNCTION

Campgrounds
1   Arrowhead RV Park   2 Van Buren Lane   (518) 382-8966

MAP 31   SCHENECTADY

B&B's / Inns / Hostels
1   A Room with a View B&B   4605 Mariaville Road   (518) 377-1699
2   Glen Sanders Mansion   1 Glen Avenue   (518) 374-7262
3   The Stockade Inn   1 North Church Street   (518) 346-3400
4   English Garden B&B   205 Union Street   (518) 372-4390
5   Widow Kendall House   10 North Ferry Street   (518) 370-5511
6   Van Voast House B&B   1353 Union Street   (518) 393-1634

Hotels / Motels
1   L&M Motel   2 Rice Road   (518) 372-5731
2   Parker Inn   434 State Street   (518) 688-1001
3   Holiday Inn Holidome   100 Nott Terrace   (518) 393-4141
4   Days Inn Schenectady   167 Nott Terrace   (518) 370-DAYS
5   Malozzi's Belvedere Hotel   1926 Curry Road   (518) 630-4020

Campgrounds
1   Frosty Acres   5 Skyline Road   (518) 864-5606

MAP 32   COHOES-WATERFORD

B&B's / Inns / Hostels
1   Old Judge Mansion   3300 Sixth Avenue   (518) 274-5698

Hotels / Motels
1   Hilton Garden Inn   800 Albany-Shaker Road   (518) 464-4666
2   Comfort Inn Albany Airport   866 Albany Shaker Road   (518) 783-1900
3   The Desmond   660 Albany Shaker Road   (518) 869-8100
3   Wingate Inn   254 Old Wolf Road   (518) 869-9100
4   Holiday Inn Turf   205 Wolf Road   (518) 458-7250
4   Courtyard by Marriot   168 Wolf Road   (518) 482-8800
4   Best Western Airport Inn   200 Wolf Road   (518) 458-1000
4   Susse Chalet   44 Wolf Road   (518) 459-5670
4   Red Roof Inn   188 Wolf Road   (518) 459-1970
4   Days Inn Albany Airport   16 Wolf Road   (518) 459-3600
4   Coccas Inn and Suites   2 Wolf Road   (518) 459-2240

5	Clarion Inn and Suites	611 Troy-Schenectady Road	(518) 785-5891
6	Microtel	7 Rensselaer Avenue	(518) 782-9161
7	Hampton Inn	981 New Loudon Road	(518) 785-0000

MAP 33   TROY-ALBANY

B&B's / Inns / Hostels

| 1 | Pine Haven B&B | 531 Western Avenue | (518) 482-1574 |

Hotels / Motels

1	Franklin Square Inn and Suites	1 Fourth Street	(518) 274-8800
2	Best Western Rensselaer Inn	1800 6th Avenue	(518) 274-3210
3	Woods Lodge	8 Crumitie Road	(518) 532-7529
4	Red Carpet Inn	500 Northern Boulevard	(518) 462-5562
5	Motel 6	100 Watervliet Avenue	(518) 438-7447
6	Quality Inn Albany	3 Watervliet Avenue	(518) 438-8431
7	Best Western Regency	416 Southern Boulevard	(518) 462-6555
8	Econo Lodge	110 Columbia Turnpike	(518) 472-1360

MAP 33A   DOWNTOWN ALBANY

B&B's / Inns / Hostels

1	The Kittleman House	70 Willett Street (518) 432-3979	
2	Morgan State House	393 State Street	(518) 427-6063
3	State Street Mansion	281 State Street (Bleecker Café)	(518) 462-6780
4	Albany Mansion Hill Inn	115 Phillip Street	(518) 465-2038

Hotels / Motels

| 1 | Crowne Plaza Albany | State and Lodge streets | (518) 462-6611 |
| 2 | Ramada Albany Downtown | 300 Broadway | (518) 434-4111 |

One of the many charming
B&B's located along the route

BICYCLE SHOPS

An asterisk* denotes rentals available

MAP 1   BUFFALO SOUTH

1	Bicycles & More	2474 George Urban Boulevard	(716) 683-1250
2	Campus Wheelworks	744 Elmwood Avenue	(716) 881-3613
3	Mangione Hardware	448 Niagara Street	(716) 847-6414

MAP 1A   DOWNTOWN BUFFALO

1*	Rick's Cycle Shop	743 Main Street	(716) 852-6838

MAP 2   BUFFALO NORTH

1	Dick's Bicycle Shop	781 River Road	(716) 694-9232
2	Handlebars Cycle Co.	685 Englewood Avenue	(716) 835-0334
3	Shickluna Bike & Fitness	1835 Hertel Avenue	(716) 837-6122
4*	Campus Wheelworks	744 Elmwood Avenue	(716) 881-3613
5	Mangione Hardware	448 Niagara Street	(716) 847-6414

MAP 3   TONAWANDAS

1	Dave's Classic Bicycles	3302 Niagara Falls Boulevard	(716) 694-0167
2	Niagara Cycle Works	1246 Payne Avenue	(716) 692-8211
3	Bert's Bikes & Sports	1550 Niagara Falls Boulevard	(716) 837-4882

MAP 4   LOCKPORT

1	North Star Bikes & Sports	5891 South Transit Road	(716) 434-9036

MAP 8   BROCKPORT-SPENCERPORT

1*	Bicycle Outfitters	72 Main Street	(585) 637-9901
2*	Sugar's Bike Shop	2139 North Union Street	(585) 352-8300

MAP 9   ROCHESTER WEST

1	Sugar's Bike Shop	2139 North Union Street	(585) 352-8300
2	Bicycle Co.	2586 West Ridge Road	(585) 453-9260
3	Bike Man	172 Driving Park Avenue	(585) 254-4352
4	Freewheelers	1757 Mount Hope Road	(585) 473-3724

MAP 9A   DOWNTOWN ROCHESTER

1	Towner's	1048 University Avenue	(585) 271-4553

MAP 10   ROCHESTER EAST

1	Freewheelers	1757 Mount Hope Road	(585) 473-3724
2	Park Avenue Bike Shop	600 Jay Scutti Boulevard	(585) 427-2110
3	Pedallers Bike Shop Ltd.	2511 East Henrietta Road	(585) 334-1083
4*	Towpath Bike Shop	7 Schoen Place	(585) 381-2808
5*	RV&E Bike & Skate	40 North Main Street	(585) 388-1350

MAP 11   FAIRPORT-PALMYRA

1*	RV&E Bike & Skate	40 North Main Street	(585) 388-1350

MAP 16   PORT BYRON-WEEDSPORT
1   Bicycles Today   360 Grant Avenue (Auburn)   (315) 253-9958

MAP 18   SYRACUSE WEST
1   Advance Cyclery   118 Seeley Road, #2   (315) 449-2453
2   Waynes & Meltzers
    Bike Super Store   2714 Erie Boulevard East   (315) 449-4607

MAP 19   SYRACUSE EAST
1   Ski Co.   3401 Erie Boulevard East   (315) 445-1890
2* Open Road Sports   3530 Erie Boulevard East   (315) 446-3287
3   Lund's Ski Shop   6820 East Genesee Street   (315) 445-0880
4   Dewitt Sports   6901 East Genesee Street   (315) 446-0460

MAP 22   ROME
1* Schuss Ski & Bicycle Shop   811 Black River Boulevard North   (315) 337-4320

MAP 23   ORISKANY
1* Schuss Ski & Bike   4610 Commercial Drive   (315) 736-1129
2   Dick Sonne's Cycling & Fitness   4465 Commercial Drive   (315) 736-7106

MAP 24   UTICA-FRANKFORT
1* Welch's Bicycle & Ski   1048 Whitesboro Street   (315) 724-4728
2* Welch's Bicycle & Ski   28 Auburn Avenue   (315) 724-5999

MAP 25   ILION-HERKIMER
1   Dick's Wheel Shop   411 Mohawk Street   (315) 866-5571

MAP 28   CANAJOHARIE-FULTONVILLE
1   Bike Works (Johnstown)   400 N Perry Street   (518) 762-1342

MAP 31   SCHENECTADY
1   Adirondack Bicycles   279 North Ballston Avenue   (518) 374-7989
2   Freeman's Bridge Sports   38 Freemans Bridge Road   (518) 382-0593
3* Plaine & Son   1816 State Street   (518) 346-1433

MAP 32   COHOES-WATERFORD
1   Rudy's Schwinn Cyclery   578 2nd Avenue   (518) 235-2525

MAP 33   TROY-ALBANY
1   Klarsfeld's Schwinn Cyclery   1370 Central Avenue   (518) 459-3272
1   Wheel World Family Bikes   281 Sand Creek Road   (518) 459-7463
2* Sycaway Bicycle Sales & Service   13 Lord Avenue   (518) 273-7788

MAP 33A DOWNTOWN ALBANY
1* Down Tube Cycle Shop   466 Madison Avenue, #1   (518) 434-1711

FAIRS & FESTIVALS

The Erie Canalway Trail passes through more than 200 upstate New York communities, each with its unique character and history. Festivals are a great way to sample local color. Summer is the height of the festival season, while fall heralds many harvest festivals. The Erie Canal corridor is also home to the New York State Fair and many county fairs that celebrate the agricultural heritage and bounty of upstate New York.

Contact nearby visitor information centers for more information and to confirm dates and locations of the fairs and festivals listed below.

MAY

Tulip Fest
First full weekend in May
Washington Park, Albany

CanalFest
Second Saturday in May
Harbor Visitors Center, Waterford

Lilac Festival
Middle two weeks in May
Highland Park, Rochester

Jazz Festival
Third Sunday in May
Apple Orchard Inn (1104 Route 31E), Medina

JUNE

Oz Fest
First Thursday to Sunday in June
Downtown Chittenango

Fairport Canal Days
First weekend in June
Downtown Fairport & Harbor

Allentown Art Festival
Second weekend in June
Allentown Historic District, Buffalo

Strawberry Festival
Second weekend in June
Courthouse Square, Albion

Positively Pittsford
Second Sunday in June
Main Street in Pittsford

Firemen's Carnival
Third Thursday to Sunday in June
Downtown Spencerport

Seneca Falls Canal Fest
Third weekend in June
Downtown Seneca Falls

Frankfort Days
Third full weekend in June
Downtown Frankfort

Sunset Festival
Third full weekend in June
Waterfront Park, Sylvan Beach

Canal Festival Day
Third Sunday in June
Chittenango Landing & Boat Museum

JULY

Friendship Festival
July 1st to July 4th
Waterfront Parks, Buffalo (U.S.) & Fort Erie (Canada)

Steamboat Festival
First Saturday in July
Harbor Visitor's Center, Waterford

Corn Hill Arts Festival
Weekend after July 4th
Corn Hill Neighborhood, Rochester

Cayuga County Fair
Second Tuesday-Saturday in July
County Fairgrounds, Weedsport

Peppermint Days
Second Thursday-Monday in July
Downtown Lyons

Taste of Buffalo
Second weekend in July
Main Street (Church to Chippewa Streets), Buffalo

Schoharie Crossing Canal Days
Second weekend in July
Schoharie Crossing State Historic Site, Fort Hunter

Fleet Bluesfest
Second weekend in July
Empire State Plaza, Albany

Convention Days
Third Thursday to Sunday in July
Downtown Seneca Falls

Hill Cumorah Pageant
Second full weekend plus one week in July
Hill Cumorah Center, Palmyra

Seneca County Fair
Third Tuesday-Saturday in July
County Fairgrounds, Waterloo

Canal Fest of the Tonawandas
Third to fourth Sunday in July
Gateway Park and Downtown, Tonawanda & North Tonawanda

Rhythm and Blues Festival
Third weekend in July
Clinton Square Neighborhood in Syracuse

Jazz Fest
Third Saturday and Sunday in July
Waterfront Park in Sylvan Beach

Annual Ilion Days
Third and Fourth weekends in July
Downtown Ilion

Monroe County Fair
Fourth Wednesday-Sunday in July
Monroe County Fairgrounds, Henrietta

Canal Days
Last full weekend in July
Downtown Spencerport

AUGUST

Fleet Waterfest
First weekend in August
Erie Basin Marina, Buffalo

Lovejoy's Iron Island Festival
First weekend in August
Lovejoy Street, Buffalo

Niagara County Fair
First weekend in August
County Fairgrounds, Niagara Falls

Cobblestone Fair
First Saturday in August
Cobblestone Society Museum, Albion

Port Byron Canal Days
First weekend in August
Downtown Port Byron

Park Ave Summer Arts Fest
First Monday and Tuesday in August
Park Avenue & S. Goodman Street, Rochester

Wayne County Fair
Second Monday-Saturday in August
Wayne County Fairgrounds, Palmyra

Herkimer County Fair
Second Tuesday-Sunday in August
County Fairgrounds, Frankfort

Brockport Arts Festival
Second weekend in August
Downtown Brockport

Canalfest
Second weekend in August
Downtown Sylvan Beach

Canal Celebration
Second weekend in August
Downtown Little Falls

Altamont Fair
Third Tuesday through Sunday in August
Fairgrounds, Altamont

Montgomery County Fair
Fourth Tuesday-Sunday in August
County Fairgrounds, Fonda

Buffalo Wing Festival
Last full weekend of August
Dunn Tire Park, Buffalo

New York State Fair
Twelve days before Labor Day
State Fairgrounds, Syracuse

SEPTEMBER

Clothesline Festival
First weekend in September
University of Rochester Memorial Art Gallery

Tugboat Roundup
Weekend after Labor Day
Harbor Visitors Center, Waterford

Oktoberfest
Second and Third weekend in September
Camp Eastman Park, Irondequoit

Canaltown Days
Second weekend in September
Downtown Palmyra

Golden Harvest Festival
Second weekend in September
Beaver Lake Nature Center, Baldwinsville

Jazz Fest
Second weekend in September
Corning Riverfront Preserve, Albany

Madison County Hop Festival
Third weekend in September
Madison County Historical Society, Oneida

Taste of the Arts
Third weekend in September
Downtown Rome

Lark Fest
Third Saturday in September
Lark Street (Between Washington & Madison Avenues), Albany

SPECIAL / ONGOING

Cycling The Erie Canal
Second week of July
Buffalo to Albany supported bike ride
Parks & Trails New York

Historic Train Trips
May through December
Railroad Museum, Medina

Concerts on the Canal
Wednesday and Friday evenings from June through August
Gateway Park, North Tonawanda

Music & Cruise Nights
Friday evenings from June through August
Canal Harbor, Medina

Concerts at the Gazebo
Sunday evenings from June through August
Canal Harbor Gazebo, Spencerport

Orchard Train Rides
July through October
Watts Farms Country Market, Albion

CYCLING SAFETY

Exploring the Erie Canalway Trail route by bicycle will mean riding on public roads as well as on off-road trails. Following are suggestions for safe and enjoyable cycling.

Wear a helmet

Cyclists are strongly encouraged to wear a helmet. Each year nearly 70,000 bicyclists suffer serious head injuries. While wearing a helmet does not prevent accidents, research shows that bicycle helmets can prevent three out of four serious cycling head injuries.

In New York State, riders age 1-13 are <u>required</u> to wear an approved helmet. Passengers age 1-4 must wear a helmet and ride in a child seat. No passengers under the age of 1 are permitted on a bicycle.

Your helmet should sit flat atop your head, fit snugly, not obstruct your view, and be approved by the Consumer Product Safety Commission (CPSC), the American Society for Testing and Materials (ASTM), or the Snell Memorial Foundation.

Follow rules of the road

Cyclists in New York State have the same responsibilities as motorists and are required to follow all traffic regulations. Riders can make their trips safer by observing some basic traffic rules.
- Stop at red lights, obey all posted signs, and follow lane markings.
- Ride right with traffic. Do not ride on sidewalks.
- When turning, use turn lanes and proper hand signals.
- Don't pass on the right. Cars and trucks have blind spots, especially in the right rear corner.
- Never wear headphones while cycling.

See and be seen

As a cyclist, you are a part of a complex traffic environment and cannot assume that motor vehicles will always yield to you. Be aware of your surroundings and make yourself visible to motorists.
- Always ride where approaching and passing motorists can see you.
- Wear bright-colored clothing during the day and reflective clothing or patches at night.
- Mount reflectors on wheels, pedals, and other surfaces.

- New York State law requires that bicyclists use both front and rear lights at night. The headlight should be visible from at least 500 feet and the taillight from 300 feet.
- Stay aware of traffic around you. Make eye contact with motorists and pedestrians at intersections and when merging.

Some additional cycling safety and comfort considerations

- Ride a bike that is the right size and correctly adjusted for you.
- Keep your bike in good repair. Check brakes and tires regularly.
- Watch out for hazards in the road. Avoid parallel-slat sewer grates, potholes, gravel, sand, ice, and debris.
- Dress appropriately. Layers allow you to adjust to temperature changes. In rain, wear a poncho or waterproof suit.
- On long trips and hot days, prevent dehydration by drinking plenty of fluids.

TRAIL ETIQUETTE

The Erie Canalway Trail is a multi-use trail and is used for walking, hiking, jogging, cycling, in-line skating, cross-country skiing, and, where permitted, horseback riding and riding snowmobiles. Help make everyone's trail experience pleasant by following accepted trail etiquette.

- **Wheels yield to heels.** Cyclists stay to the right and yield the right of way to all other trail users.
- **Signal when passing.** Give a courteous audible warning when passing pedestrians and other bicyclists.
- **Maintain control of your speed.** Approach turns anticipating someone around the bend. Be able to stop safely within the distance you can see down the trail.
- **Don't block the trail.** When in a group, use no more than half the trail, so as not to block the flow of other users.
- **Stay on the trail.** Avoid trespassing on private land and trampling vegetation. Work is ongoing to improve and expand the Canalway Trail; respect trail and road closure and detour signs.
- **Do not disturb wildlife or livestock.** Avoid sudden movements, loud noises, and unexpected approaches that can startle animals and be dangerous to you and others.
- **Leave No Trace.** Carry out what you carry in.
- **Be respectful.** Be respectful of other trail users regardless of their speed or skill level.
- **Follow all posted regulations.** Many different state, county, and municipal agencies manage segments of the Canalway Trail; their rules and regulations sometimes differ.

TRAVEL AND LOGISTICS

Travel options abound along the Erie Canalway Trail corridor. Following are a few ideas to help you devise a plan that works for you.

Distances

You're never very far from "civilization" on the Erie Canalway Trail. The following chart provides distances between some of the larger communities along the route.

	Albany	Albion	Amsterdam	Brockport	Buffalo	Canajoharie & Palatine Bridge	Canastota	Depew	Fairport	Little Falls	Lockport	Newark	Rochester	Rome	Schenectady & Scotia	Seneca Falls	Syracuse	Tonawanda & North Tonawanda	Utica	Weedsport
Albany		319	46	305	379	68	149	389	273	89	347	252	287	127	29	222	174	366	111	198
Albion	319		273	14	60	251	170	70	46	230	28	67	32	192	290	97	145	47	208	121
Amsterdam	46	273		259	333	22	103	343	227	43	301	206	241	81	17	176	128	320	65	152
Brockport	305	14	259		74	237	156	84	32	216	42	53	18	178	276	83	131	61	194	107
Buffalo	379	60	333	74		311	230	10	106	290	32	127	92	252	350	157	205	13	268	181
Canajoharie & Palatine Bridge	68	251	22	237	311		81	321	205	21	279	184	219	59	39	154	106	298	43	130
Canastota	149	170	103	156	230	81		240	124	60	198	103	138	22	120	73	25	217	38	49
Depew	389	70	343	84	10	321	240		116	300	42	137	102	262	360	167	215	23	278	191
Fairport	273	46	227	32	106	205	124	116		184	74	21	14	146	244	51	99	93	162	75
Little Falls	89	230	43	216	290	21	60	300	184		258	163	198	38	60	133	85	277	22	109
Lockport	347	28	301	42	32	279	198	42	74	258		95	60	220	318	125	173	19	236	149
Newark	252	67	206	53	127	184	103	137	21	163	95		35	125	223	30	78	114	141	54
Rochester	287	32	241	18	92	219	138	102	14	198	60	35		160	258	65	113	79	176	89
Rome	127	192	81	178	252	59	22	262	146	38	220	125	160		98	95	47	239	16	71
Schenectady & Scotia	29	290	17	276	350	39	120	360	244	60	318	223	258	98		193	145	337	82	169
Seneca Falls	222	97	176	83	157	154	73	167	51	133	125	30	65	95	193		48	144	111	24
Syracuse	174	145	128	131	205	106	25	215	99	85	173	78	113	47	145	48		192	63	24
Tonawanda & North Tonawanda	366	47	320	61	13	298	217	23	93	277	19	114	79	239	337	144	192		255	168
Utica	111	208	65	194	268	43	38	278	162	22	236	141	176	16	82	111	63	255		87
Weedsport	198	121	152	107	181	130	49	191	75	109	149	54	89	71	169	24	24	168	87	

Renting a bike

For spur of the moment trips in which you just want to experience a taste of cycling along the Erie Canal, renting a bicycle is a good option. The bike shop listing in this guide indicates which shops offer rentals.

Transporting your bike

The Erie Canal corridor offers four main travel modes: air, rail, bus, and car. Unless you rent a bike locally, the first three of these require that you make special preparations to travel with your bicycle. Usually, this means breaking down your bicycle so that it will fit into a standard bike-shipping box (available at most bicycle and shipping stores). Preparing a bicycle for a shipping box typically entails removing the pedals and re-attaching them on the inside of the crankshaft and turning the handlebar so it is parallel with the wheel.

If you're willing to spend a few extra dollars, it might make sense to ship your bicycle directly to your first night's lodging so that you only have to deal with your regular luggage during travel.

If you aren't comfortable breaking down and re-assembling your bicycle, consider having it shipped from a bike shop near you to a bike shop near your starting point. This service falls outside a bike shop's typical activities, so be prepared to pay a reasonable fee.

Plane

Four major well-spaced airports (Buffalo – BUF; Rochester – ROC; Syracuse – SYR; and Albany – ALB) operate along the Erie Canal corridor, providing a gateway to each of the four sections defined in this guide. Each airport is no more than a 20-minute taxi ride from the Erie Canalway Trail. Bear in mind that commercial airlines usually charge an extra fee to transport bicycles.

If you plan to complete the length of the trail route and travel by plane, it's advisable to fly into Buffalo and out of Albany (or vice-versa). If two one-way flights are too expensive or not allowed from your embarkation location, consider flying round-trip to your starting location and using train or bus transportation to travel back to your starting point.

Train

Nine Amtrak stations serve the Erie Canal Corridor: Buffalo-Exchange St., Buffalo-Depew St., Rochester, Syracuse, Rome, Utica, Amsterdam, Schenectady, and Albany-Rensselaer.

New York State is fortunate in that it hosts two of only four Amtrak routes on the East Coast (the north-south Adirondack and the Ethan Allen Express routes) that offer bike roll-on/roll-off baggage car service. Unfortunately, Albany is the only city along the Erie Canal corridor served by these two routes. However, if you're from Vermont or the New York City area and riding the trail westward to Albany, this might be a good option for you. If you're able to take advantage of this service, you must reserve baggage space in advance and pay a small additional fee.

The primary Amtrak route serving the canal corridor is the Empire Service. It requires that your bike be boxed for baggage car transport. The downtown Buffalo Station (Exchange Street) does not have baggage-handling service, however, so you must debark east of downtown Buffalo at the Depew Station. From there, you can ride or take a taxi or bus (via Route 6/bikes only allowed during off-peak hours) to the start of the trail.

Considering all this, if you plan to travel by train, it might be easier to ship your bike ahead of time to your first-night lodging.

If you would like traveling on Amtrak with a bike to be easier, please contact Amtrak and request that bike roll-on/roll-off service be instituted along the Erie Canal corridor.

Automobile

If you're coming from a relatively short distance, the most convenient way to access the Erie Canalway Trail is probably by car. For a family or group living in or near New York State, it's also likely to be the most economical way.

For those not traveling solo, using two vehicles offers several options. The simplest option is to drop one vehicle at your planned destination, then drive, with your bikes and luggage, in the other car to your starting point. At the end of your trip, drive back to retrieve the other car. This approach works for both single- and multi-day trips. Remember to keep both sets of keys with you!

If you're planning to travel the entire length of the trail, however, this method means a long drive to retrieve the second car at the end of your trip. Another option is to send one or two people back to the first car via Amtrak (the rest of the group should treat them to dinner when they return!) while everyone else enjoys a day exploring the local area. This works particularly well if you park the first car at an Amtrak station.

A more complex variation of the car-drop approach for a multi-day trip is to take two cars, but instead of dropping one car at your ultimate destination, drop it at each day's end point. At the end of a day's riding, drive back to where the first car is parked, drive both cars to the day's end point, then drive one car out to the next day's destination. The benefits of this car-hopping method are that you always have a car with you in the evening, you can use day-use parking areas, and your second car is close by at the end of your trip. The downside is that you must spend hours each day driving.

When dropping off cars as part of a multi-day trip, park at well-used, secure locations, such as an Amtrak station or a parking lot with long-term rates. If you're starting or ending your journey at a hotel, motel, or B&B, you might inquire if you can park your car there.

Solo travelers and groups with only one car can combine driving with return trips on the bus or train. A convenient arrangement is to drive to your starting point and park at an Amtrak station. Ride the trail to another community with an Amtrak station. Store your bicycle in a secure spot (such as your room, if you're staying in a motel or B&B). Take the train back to your car and drive back to where your bike is stored.

The ideal scenario for cyclists is to have a support or 'sag' vehicle shadowing them as a backup for food, equipment, and emergencies. If you have a non-cycling travel partner or members of your group willing to rotate in the support role, they can drive the vehicle while others bicycle. Two-way radios or cell phones are helpful when using this approach.

Car rental

Renting a car is a less than ideal option because one-way rentals tend to be more expensive than round-trip rentals. Also, many rental companies don't allow bike racks to be mounted on their vehicles. If you do rent a car, ask for a model with back seats that fold down so you can expand the trunk room to accommodate bicycles.

Baggage shuttle

For those who plan to travel from B&B to B&B and who like to travel light, call ahead to see if you can arrange for your luggage to be shuttled between destinations. That way, you only need to carry what you require for the day — rain jacket, tool kit, first-aid kit, food, water, camera, and other accessories.

A few organized tours along the canal corridor provide baggage shuttle and other support services. Additionally, some B&B owners have begun coordinating amongst themselves to provide this service to individuals and small groups. You may very well be able to find a chain of owners willing to carry your luggage. Expect to pay a fee for this service, of course.

Parks & Trails New York runs an annual 500-person cycling trip along the Erie Canal from Buffalo to Albany each July. Visit www.ptny.org for more information on *Cycling the Erie Canal*.

PREPARING FOR MULTI-DAY CYCLING TRIPS

Conditioning

Attaining a basic fitness level and comfort in the saddle before starting out will make your trip more enjoyable. Begin your preparations several weeks ahead of time and build slowly, especially if you haven't cycled in a while. *It's always a good idea to consult with your physician before starting any exercise program.*

Some training is better than none. Set a reasonable goal, given your schedule, and stick to it. Start with 5-mile bike rides and, when you're comfortable, increase to 10-mile rides. Continue adding 5-mile increments until you are in the 30-mile range. Then, test your endurance by doing a 40- or 50-mile ride.

Take rides with loaded racks or panniers to get accustomed to the extra weight and change in balance. By the time you start your trip, you should be comfortable spending at least four hours at a time in the saddle. Get to know your body's food and hydration needs during long rides so that you can prepare for them in advance.

If you plan to take children, it's essential to include them in the training plan. Use training trips to teach children to drink plenty of water, to eat regularly, and to follow the rules of the road and trail. Spend time honing their skills (and yours) in riding in traffic. If you plan to carry small children in trailers or bike seats, use conditioning rides to test their comfort and endurance.

You might find it helpful to seek out a local cycling club for training advice and for opportunities to participate in group rides. You'll not only pick up many riding and equipment tips but you'll meet some great people who share your interest in cycling.

Equipment

Having the right equipment and gear makes a big difference. Following are some basic equipment suggestions.

Bicycle

Your bicycle is the most critical piece of equipment for cycling the Erie Canalway Trail. Therefore, it's essential that it be both comfortable and reliable.

Newer, higher-end bikes tend to be lighter and easier to ride, but older bicycles can certainly do the job. A wide selection of gears will help reduce fatigue. New or old, your bike should be in top mechanical condition and properly fitted and adjusted to you. Most bike shops can perform a detailed inspection and tune-up, as well as adjust your bike for proper fit, for around $75.

Hybrid-type bicycles or mountain bikes without knobby tire treads are recommended for the different trail surfaces and on-road sections of the Canalway Trail route. If you must use a racing or touring bike, use tires with a minimum width of 1.5 inches. Consult your local bicycle shop for options.

Even if you are traveling light, without camping gear or overnight baggage, you will still find some sort of handlebar bag or pannier convenient to carry extra clothes, snacks, and other accessories. Panniers should attach securely to your bicycle frame to avoid weight shifting and interference with your chain or wheels.

New York State Law requires use of a light by anyone riding a bicycle on public roads at night. The new LED lights combine long battery life with strong illumination.

It's important to stay hydrated during a cycling trip. Have at least two water bottle cages or holders attached to your bike frame or use a handlebar bag or panniers that can carry several water bottles. A camelback water container, which is worn like a backpack, is also an option.

Since you will most likely stop often at points of interest, shops, and restaurants along the route, take a sturdy bike lock. An easily detachable gear bag allows you to take your more valuable items with you when you leave your bike.

Clothing

To stay comfortable during a long cycling trip, your clothing
must perform three functions: keep you dry, block wind, and
cushion pressure points (hands and posterior).

Your body controls its temperature through perspiration.
Therefore, clothing that allows perspiration to easily evaporate
will keep you dry and cool on hot days and dry and warm on
cold days. Generally, cotton does this poorly (though in warm,
dry weather it's fine) because it absorbs and holds a lot of
moisture. Modern synthetic fibers help 'wick' moisture
away from skin to a garment's exterior. Clothing made from
synthetic materials also dries quickly so you can wash it at
night in a sink and usually wear it the next day.

Most bicycle jerseys and shorts are made from synthetic
materials, allowing the breeze you generate as you ride to
sweep away your perspiration and keep you cool in warmer
temperatures. In cooler temperatures, the breeze from riding
becomes an undesirable wind chill, forcing your body to strain
to generate enough heat for your muscles to function efficiently.
To compensate, add bulk through additional clothing layers
or add a windproof shell or both. In very cool temperatures,
it's also advisable to wear cycling tights or windproof pants.
Invest in synthetic undergarments to take full advantage of
the 'wicking' phenomenon.

Layering allows you to adjust to a range of conditions.
Remember that it can cool down significantly at night in
upstate New York, especially in the spring and fall.

Rain will lower your body temperature even more quickly than wind so a good rain jacket is critical. Rain pants are also a good idea. Rain ponchos are not as good as jackets because they tend to billow while riding. In a pinch, a garbage bag with holes cut out for arms and head can help protect your body's core.

Water-resistant is not the same as waterproof. Water-resistant jackets will soak through in an extended rainstorm. Higher-end rain jackets use a waterproof and "breathable" coating that allows your perspiration to evaporate. Waterproof jackets and pants are also usually windproof so they can double as wind protection.

As you ride, the entire weight of your body presses onto your bike in three areas of contact: hands, feet, and posterior. Padded bicycle gloves help ease hand pressure and chafing as well as absorb vibrations from the front tire. Synthetic cycling socks can ease the pressure on the balls of your feet while pedaling. Using an additional thin liner sock can further keep your feet dry and reduce blisters.

Many cyclists use special bicycle shoes, but the stiffer clip-in varieties can be inconvenient as you stop and visit the attractions and communities along the trail. If you do opt for a bicycle shoe, sneaker-type ones will allow you to more comfortably walk longer distances.

Padded lycra bicycling shorts are a must for longer trips. If you feel awkward about their appearance, you can wear a loose-fitting pair of regular shorts over them or purchase special bike touring shorts that have the appearance of normal shorts but are constructed with a pad.

Basic Bike Tool Kit

Many bicycle tool kits are commercially available, but you can easily assemble your own. Essential tool kit ingredients:
- Spare tube, tube patch kit, tire lever
- Small frame pump
- Open end wrenches
- Allen wrenches
- Screwdrivers
- Chain tool, chain lube, extra chain links
- Small pliers / multi-purpose tool
- Zip ties or bailing wire
- Bungee cords
- Duct tape

First Aid/Emergency Kit

The benefits of carrying a small first aid kit far outweigh the disadvantage of a little extra weight. Basic first aid kit ingredients:

- Bandages (assorted sizes, including triangular)
- Adhesive tape
- Antiseptic ointment
- Gauze pads and roller gauze (assorted sizes)
- Scissors and tweezers
- Small flashlight and extra batteries
- Swiss army knife or small folding knife
- Matches and candle

Other Useful Accessories

- Cell phone
- Sunglasses
- Camera & film
- Pad & pen
- Weather radio
- Fanny pack
- HALT spray (to keep dogs away)
- Sunscreen
- Insect repellant

ADDITIONAL READING AND RESOURCES

Route Guides

Along the Bike Hike-Trail, Schenectady County
Environmental Clearinghouse of Schenectady

Along the Bike-Hike Trail: A Guide to the Canalway Trail in Montgomery County by Patricia Rush & Patrick Clear
Environmental Clearinghouse of Schenectady

Canal Cruising Guide by New York State Canal Corporation
Northern Cartographic

Cycling Along the Canals of New York by Louis Rossi
Vitesse Press

Erie Canal Bicyclist & Hiker Route Guide by Harvey Botzman
Cyclotour Guide Books

Erie Canal: Canoeing America's Great Waterway by Peter Lourie
Boyds Mill Press

*Inn to Inn Touring Along the Erie Canal-Western
and Eastern Sections*
New York State Canal Corporation/Parks & Trails New York

The New Erie Canal by John R. Fitzgerald
Quest Press

History

A Long Haul by Michele McFee
Purple Mountain Press

*The Artificial River: the Erie Canal and the Paradox
of Progress, 1817–1862* by Carol Sheriff
Hill & Wang

The Erie Canal: The Ditch That Opened A Nation by Dan Murphy
Western New York Wares

Erie Water West: A History of the Erie Canal by Ronald Shaw
University Press of Kentucky

The Long Haul West by Madeline Waggoner
G.P. Putnams Sons

New York State Canals, A Short History by F. Daniel Larkin
Purple Mountain Press

Stars In The Water: The Story of the Erie Canal by George Condon
Doubleday

The Story of the New York State Canals by Roy G. Finch
J.B. Lyon Company

Waterway West: The Story of the Erie Canal by Mary Kay Phelan
Crowell

Canal Culture

Erie Canal Legacy: Architectural Treasures of the Empire State
by Andy Olenick & Richard O. Reisem
Landmark Society of Western New York

The Erie Canal Reader by Roger W. Hecht
Syracuse University Press

Children

Amazing Impossible Erie Canal by Cheryl Harness
Doubleday

CANALWAY PARTNERS

The Canalway Trail is one part of broader vision for a revitalized New York State Canal System and corridor. Many organizations and governmental entities are working with a common purpose to realize this vision.

NEW YORK STATE CANAL CORPORATION

The New York State Canal Corporation oversees the operation, maintenance and promotion of the 524-mile New York State Canal System and more than 240 miles of Canalway Trail. Its objective is to enhance land and waterside amenities, maintain historic integrity of the waterway, land and structures, and offer visitors a wide variety of unique vacation options. Designated as the nation's 23rd National Heritage Corridor, the New York State Canal System joins the ranks of America's most historic treasures.

Today, the Erie Canalway Trail is more than 60% complete and offers multiple uses, from cycling, hiking and horseback riding to snowmobiling and cross-country skiing. When finished, the 348-mile Erie Canalway Trail will be the longest multi-use recreational trail in the United States, providing extensive close-to-home recreational opportunities, linking historical and unique attractions, and serving as a destination for long distance bicycle and hiking tourism. For further information: www.canals.state.ny.us

PARKS & TRAILS NEW YORK

Parks & Trails New York (formerly New York Parks and Conservation Association) is a statewide non-profit membership organization that works to expand, protect, and promote a network of parks, trails, and open spaces throughout the state for use and enjoyment by all. To make this network a reality, Parks & Trails New York guides the development of local, grassroots groups and fosters partnerships amongst trail and park stakeholders.

As a partner in the Canalway Trail Partnership, Parks & Trails New York is working with the New York State Canal Corporation to create a continuous 524-mile trail along New York State's historic canal system. Parks & Trails New York has published 11 Canalway Trail gap segment reports designed to assist state and local agencies in routing the trail. The organization annually organizes *Cycling the Erie Canal*, a 500-person cross-state bicycle trip along the Erie Canal, to promote completion of the Canalway Trail and bicycle and heritage tourism. For more information: www.ptny.org.

ERIE CANALWAY NATIONAL HERITAGE CORRIDOR

Almost 200 years since its construction was first proposed, the Erie Canal retains genuine national significance. The U.S. Congress recognized this significance by designating the Erie Canalway National Heritage Corridor in 2000 and establishing a 27-member, citizen-based Canalway Commission. Working through a wide range of partnerships, the Commission is striving to preserve and interpret our nation's past, provide world class recreational and educational opportunities, foster economic revitalization, and improve the quality of life in over 230 corridor communities.

As of 2004, Congress has designated only two-dozen heritage areas or corridors around the country. Each one is distinctive and illustrates a significant chapter in the American experience. The Erie Canalway National Heritage Corridor is not only a monument to the past, but a living tradition. Its residents are proud of their heritage and many have worked for years to preserve their community's distinctive qualities. Through preservation and interpretation of this national treasure, the Erie Canalway National Heritage Corridor can once again serve as a key destination and as a source of economic vitality for upstate New York. For further information: www.eriecanalway.org.

CANALWAY TRAILS ASSOCIATION OF NEW YORK

The Canalway Trails Association of New York (CTANY) is a volunteer organization that works with citizens, municipalities, counties, and state agencies to maintain the Canalway Trail as a world-class multi-use recreational trail. CTANY promotes the completion and proper maintenance of the Canalway Trail and coordinates an Adopt-a-Trail Program. Adopt-a-Trail groups help care for the Canalway Trail in their communities by undertaking many types of maintenance tasks, including litter pick-up, mowing, trimming, raking, patching the trail surface, painting, landscaping, and maintaining signs. For more information about CTANY or the Adopt-a-Trail program, contact Parks & Trails New York: 518-434-1583 or canaltrail@ptny.org.

Bed and Breakfasts listed adhere to the standards of cleanliness, hospitality and professionalism of the Empire State Bed & Breakfast Association. Comfortable beds, hot showers and sumptuous breakfasts offered by people who are familiar with area resources and sites to expand your experience.

For more information, contact the innkeepers using the information listed here, or visit the ESBBA web site at www.esbba.com

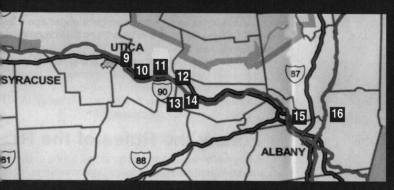

9 Pratt Smith House
10497 Cosby Manor Rd.
Deerfield, NY 13502
315-732-8483
alannem@borg.com

10 Bellinger Rose B & B
611 W. German St.
Herkimer, NY 13350
866-867-2197
bellingerrose@hotmail.com

11 The Gansevoort House B & B
42 W. Gansevoort St.
Little Falls, NY 13365
315-823-1833
lstivala@twcny.rr.com

12 INn by the Mill
1679 Mill Road
St. Johnsville, NY 13452-3911
866-568-2388
romance@innbythemill.com

13 Hazelnut Farm Bed & Breakfast
205 Paris Road
Fort Plain, NY 13339
518-993-3346
arthur@telenet.net

14 A White Rose Bed & Breakfast
105 Reid St. (Rt. 80)
Fort Plain, NY 13339
518-993-3339
awhiterose@adelphia.net

15 Van Voast House Bed & Breakfast
1353 Union St.
Schenectady, NY 12308
800-810-4948
carolbnbres@msn.com

16 Olde Judge Mansion B & B
3300 Sixth Ave.
Troy, NY 12180
866-653-5834
ojm@nycap.rr.com

photo: J. McCarthy

ALBANYNOW
START HERE!

The first stop to exploring Albany is at the
Albany Heritage Area Visitors Center
Conveniently located off I-787, there are plenty of brochures and information about the region, as well as knowledgeable staff to answer questions. *But the Visitors Center holds more than brochures!*

- **Henry Hudson Planetarium**
  an official NASA Space Place!
- **Museum Gallery**
- **Guided Tours**
- **Special Events and Exhibits**
- **Gift Shop**

Open 7 days a week | (518) 434-0405 | 800-258-3582
www.albany.org | 25 Quackenbush Square, Albany, NY 12207

I♥NY ORLEANS COUNTY, NEW YORK

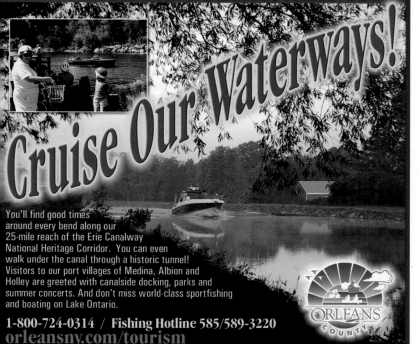

Cruise Our Waterways!

You'll find good times around every bend along our 25-mile reach of the Erie Canalway National Heritage Corridor. You can even walk under the canal through a historic tunnel! Visitors to our port villages of Medina, Albion and Holley are greeted with canalside docking, parks and summer concerts. And don't miss world-class sportfishing and boating on Lake Ontario.

1-800-724-0314 / Fishing Hotline 585/589-3220
orleansny.com/tourism

ORLEANS COUNTY

ACKNOWLEDGEMENTS

Development of *Cycling the Erie Canal* was made possible through the contributions of many individuals and organizations. We sincerely thank them all.

Steve Spindler, of BikeMap Cartography, for the beautiful maps and great patience through the drafting and design revision process.

Kelly Fahey, of Primeau-Fahey Studios, for producing a high-quality graphic design under a tight deadline.

Andy Olenick for his beautiful cover photo.

John DiMura, of the NYS Canal Corporation, who helped, whenever asked, to provide trail data and digital images and to proof draft maps.

Karl Beard, David Gaines, and **Duncan Hay** of the NPS Rivers, Trails & Conservation Assistance Program for design input, cultural resource expertise, and many thoughtful comments on content and style.

Marcia Kees and **Frank Dean** of the Erie Canalway National Heritage Corridor Commission for providing background and granting permission to use text for the history section from the National Park Service's *The Erie Canalway: An American Icon, A Summary of the New York State Canal System Special Resource Study*.

Deborah Spicer for her vision and steadfast support and **Gary Malys** and **Margaret Casey** for lending assistance at a critical time.

The many volunteer fact checkers who carefully reviewed draft maps: **Richard Grainger, Howard Halstead, Keith Kroon, Irv Perlman, Mike Riley, Carol Schmelz**, and **Alan Vincent** (Canalway Trail Association of New York), **Pat Clear** (Environmental Clearinghouse of Schenectady), Al Hastings (Cycling the Erie Canal bike tour), **Theresa LaSalle** (Capital District Transportation Committee), and **Ken Showalter** (Old Erie Canal State Historic Park).

Rachel Bliven (Mohawk Valley Heritage Corridor Commission) for sharing photos of Mohawk Valley sites and reviewing draft maps.

Frances and **George Gotcsik** for being 'model' cyclists and **Frances**, additionally, for her eagle editing eye and vital text contributions.

Josh Pierro and **Ann Cavalluzzi**, interns from the University at Albany, who did extensive research and contributed to the text. **Gregory Bell** and **Salim Adler** also made key contributions.

We wish to extend a special thank you to the New York State Canal Corporation and its employees for their dedicated and sensitive stewardship of the state's remarkable canal and canalway trail system and to Governor Pataki and the New York State Legislature for their sustained commitment to making the corridor a world class recreationway.

Photos courtesy of:

New York State Canal Corporation - Pages 8, 11, 15, 27, 29, 33, 37, 45, 47, 67, 89, 91, 93, 95, 121, 127; **New York State Department of Economic Development** - Pages 21, 23, 25, 31, 35, 39, 49, 53, 55, 63, 87, 99; **New York State Archives** - Pages 12, 13, 29, 31, 57, 79, 85; **Mohawk Valley Heritage Corridor** - Pages 69, 73, 75, 77, 83, 85, 87, 89, 135; **Parks & Trails New York** - Pages 2, 3, 9, 31, 37, 39, 41, 47, 49, 51, 53, 57, 59, 65, 69, 71, 75, 77, 83, 109, 122; **Herschell Carousel Museum** - Page 27; **Medina Railroad Museum** - Page 33; **Cobblestone Society Museum** - Page 35; **Orleans County Chamber of Commerce** - Page 35; **Buffalo Convention & Visitors Bureau** - Page 21; **Remington Firearms Museum** - Page 79; **The Canajoharie Library** - *New York and the Erie Canal* by William Wall (1862) - Page 14; **Schenectady Historical Society** - Page 91; **Chamber of Schenectady County** - Page 93; **RiverSpark Heritage Area** - Page 95, 97

Join Us!
Become a member of Parks & Trails New York today.

☐ **Yes, I want to support Parks & Trails New York's work on the Canalway Trail and its efforts to expand, protect, and promote a network of parks, trails, and open spaces throughout the state for all to use and enjoy.**

Membership Levels

☐ $15 Student/Senior   ☐ $25 Individual
☐ $35 Supporter   ☐ $50 Advocate
☐ $100 Trekker   ☐ $100 Business
☐ $250 Champion   ☐ $500 Heritage Society

Contribution

☐ Amount _____

All membership contributions are tax-deductible.

Additional Guidebook Orders

I would like _____ additional copies of *Cycling the Erie Canal* at $14.95 each, plus $3.95 shipping and handling and sales tax, where applicable, for a total of $_____.

☐ Enclosed is my check payable to PTNY

☐ Charge $ _____ to my:

    ☐ Visa   ☐ Mastercard   ☐ American Express

Account # _____

Expiration Date _____

☐ My company _____ will match my gift.

Name _____

Street Address _____

City / State / Zip _____

Daytime phone _____

E-mail address _____

Send to Parks & Trails New York
29 Elk Street • Albany, New York 12207

A copy of Parks & Trails New York's latest annual report may be obtained, upon request, from Parks & Trails New York, 29 Elk Street, Albany, NY 12207, or from the New York State Attorney General's Charities Bureau, 120 Broadway, New York, NY 10271.